200 really ea

D0069073

200 really easy recipes

hamlyn **all color**

Louise Pickford

An Hachette UK Company
www.hachette.co.uk

First published in Great Britain in 2009 by Hamlyn,
a division of Octopus Publishing Group Ltd
2–4 Heron Quays, London E14 4JP
www.octopusbooksusa.com

Copyright © Octopus Publishing Group Ltd 2009

Distributed in the U.S. and Canada by Octopus Books USA:
c/o Hachette Book Group
237 Park Avenue
New York NY 10017

Some of the recipes in this book have previously appeared
in other books published by Hamlyn.

ISBN: 978-0-600-62013-6

A CIP catalog record for this book is available from
the Library of Congress

Printed and bound in China

2 3 4 5 6 7 8 9 10

Standard level spoon measurements are used in all recipes.

Ovens should be preheated to the specified temperature—
if using a fan-assisted oven, follow the manufacturer's
instructions for adjusting the time and the temperature.

Fresh herbs should be used unless otherwise stated.

Medium eggs should be used unless otherwise stated.

The Food and Drug Administration advises that eggs should
not be consumed raw. This book contains some dishes made
with raw or lightly cooked eggs. It is prudent for vulnerable
people such as pregnant and nursing mothers, invalids, the
elderly, babies, and young children to avoid uncooked or
lightly cooked dishes made with eggs. Once prepared, these
dishes should be kept refrigerated and used promptly.

This book includes dishes made with nuts and nut
derivatives. It is advisable for those with known allergic
reactions to nuts and nut derivatives and those who may be
potentially vulnerable to these allergies to avoid dishes made
with nuts and nut oils. It is also prudent to check the labels
of pre-prepared ingredients for the possible inclusion of
nut derivatives.

contents

introduction

introduction

This book is the perfect choice for first-time cooks. It offers a wonderful collection of simple-to-prepare dishes guaranteed to make every mealtime easy. Featuring a winning combination of all-time favorites, classics with a new twist, as well as some new and exciting dishes, all the recipes have easy-to-follow methods using ingredients readily available from your local supermarket, making shopping a breeze.

Variety is the spice of life, and with so many meal ideas on offer here, you'll never be short of choice. Dishes range from tempting breakfast and brunch ideas and satisfying pasta, rice, and noodle dishes to time-saving one-pot meals (with very little washing-up) and wickedly decadent desserts. So there's something here to tempt even the most reticent cook!

Cooking is all about confidence, and the more you cook and familiarize yourself with the equipment, ingredients, and cooking methods, the easier and more enjoyable it becomes. It won't be long before you're cooking for yourself and your friends, and showing off your newfound culinary confidence!

the feel-good factor

If you're leaving home for the first time and/or starting college or a job, the experience can be rather daunting and demanding, and providing yourself and your friends with good food can seem like an extra, unwanted chore. Of course, there are many fast-food options available, but although convenient, they are often expensive and in many cases high in fat and lacking in nutritional value. If you're studying or working hard in a new job, you'll need plenty of energy to help concentration levels, so eating well is especially important, not to mention comforting! Cooking from scratch means that you have control over exactly what you eat, so you can avoid those hidden ingredients in take out and convenience foods that offer "empty" calories. Instead, you can opt for a balanced diet with lean meat and fish for protein, carbohydrates for fuel, and fresh fruit and vegetables for the essential vitamins and fiber that will keep your body's systems running smoothly. This book will provide you with nutritious as well as delicious dishes to

give you an overall sense of well-being when you need it most as well as optimum energy.

This is also a time when being in the kitchen means less time to socialize with friends and relax, so most of the dishes in this book are quick to prepare and cook—even those that are fit for a special occasion.

Just as important, however, is the satisfaction you will gain from mastering a new skill—eating well to live well!

about the recipes

The recipes are divided into seven chapters so choosing just the right dish for every occasion, is a simple and speedy process.

Breakfast is the most important meal of the day and one that often consists only of a quick caffeine fix, but this energy hit is short-lived. The range of dishes in Breakfasts &

Brunch will ensure that you have something great to eat everyday. Whether it's a healthy Summer Berry Granola, Bacon & Maple Syrup Pancakes, or the hearty Rösti with Ham & Eggs, you can get your morning off to the perfect start.

Soups & One-pot Meals provides valuable time-saving options and recipes that are also a godsend for those with a limited supply of utensils. Many recipes in this chapter make warming winter dishes, such as Beef Goulash and Chili Bean & Red Pepper Soup, when you need something more substantial to get you through chilly evenings and provide you with the necessary fuel for the following day. Leftovers can be frozen for another day, or those from other dishes such as Chicken & Rice Bake can be stored in plastic containers for satisfying packed lunches.

Working hard and playing hard often leaves little time and energy for cooking, but don't worry because 20-minute Suppers has the answer great meals in moments. Choose from a spicy Thai Chicken Curry, Italian-inspired Tuna & Pesto Burgers, or the sophisticated Lamb with Olive & Pine Nut Salsa. All the recipes in this chapter make ideal dinner party dishes, so why not impress friends and family with these sure-fire meals?

If you're studying hard at college or you've begun a new job for the first time, you'll need plenty of energy, so a chapter packed full of carbohydrate-based dishes such as those you'll find in Pasta, Rice, & Noodles will hit the spot. Fuel up on Sausage Meatballs, Peas, & Pasta, Baked Risotto with Burnt Butter, or a simple Pad Thai noodle dish.

Meat and fish are relatively expensive, but in order to maintain a healthy diet, it's essential to eat protein when we can. There are plenty of dishes in Meat, Poultry, & Fish that use cheaper cuts of meat, such as ground beef and lamb, chicken wings, and ribs. And although most fish are pricey, they are definitely worth reserving for a special occasion or a dinner party. You can also substitute cheaper kinds of fish in most of the recipes.

Vegetarian Dishes & Salads is perfect for all non meat-eaters, although there are many more meat-free dishes dotted throughout the book offering a wide variety of delicious meals. Try the Moroccan-inspired Chickpea Tagine, the aromatic Mixed Vegetable Curry, or the fancy Halloumi & Fig Pastry Pizza.

The final chapter Easy Desserts & Cakes is for those with a sweet tooth, packed full of sumptuous desserts and sweet treats for everyday as well as for entertaining. Chocolate Refrigerator Cake, for example, serves up to 30 people and keeps well, making it a perfect midmorning snack to go with coffee. There is a lovely Fruit Salad with Elderflower Syrup for the summer months, while the Sticky Toffee Puddings are ideal for winter.

pantry essentials

Keeping a well-stocked pantry is both useful and great for last minute suppers. Here are a few essential items...

Extra virgin olive oil and vegetable oil These are essential for salad dressings as well as for frying and roasting.
White wine vinegar, red wine vinegar, and balsamic vinegar These are good options for both marinating meat and poultry for more tender results and for piquant salad dressings.
Canned chopped tomatoes A must for making flavorful sauces for all kinds of dishes.
Canned tuna in olive oil It is both healthy and tasty, and can be used either cold in salads or as a spread, or served hot in a pasta sauce or made into fish cakes.

Canned chickpeas and red kidney beans
These are great for making quick salads and also for adding to soups, stews, and casseroles.

Dried pasta and noodles They are endlessly versatile, for using cold to make salads as well as for hot main meals and adding to soups. Keep a selection of different forms, such as spaghetti, penne, and fusilli pasta and rice noodles and thread and medium egg noodles.

Spices and dried herbs These can be acquired gradually, a different one each week, to build up a versatile selection, including ground cumin, coriander, and turmeric, jerk seasoning and dried red pepper flakes for adding aromatic flavor and heat; ground cinnamon for both sweet and savory dishes; dried oregano and thyme for Mediterranean flavoring.

Sea salt and whole black peppercorns These are the best options for everyday seasoning, to grind fresh for maximum flavor.

Basmati, long-grain, and risotto rice Rice adds bulk to a meal, and also makes delicious meals in its own right, such as pilafs and risottos.

All-purpose and self-rising flours These are vital for baking and for cheese or white sauce.

Superfine sugar and light and dark brown sugar These are the most versatile sugar options, the former being easiest to dissolve and the latter for adding a rich flavor.

Asian sauces Sauces such as soy, oyster, hoisin, Thai fish, and sweet chili sauce, are great for giving stir-fry, noodle, and steamed dishes an instant flavor hit.

shopping advice

Always make a shopping list before you shop. A weekly trip to the supermarket is perfect for nonperishables, but if you can, shop daily for fresh ingredients from a local butcher, fish merchant, or vegetable store as they can help advise you on the best and cheapest seasonal ingredients.

Although supermarkets have a fast turnover of fresh meat and fish, always check the "sell by" and "use by" dates on the labels and only buy produce that looks fresh and vibrant rather than tired. Butchers will often sell you a single steak or chop, whereas supermarkets tend to offer cheaper, bulk-buying opportunities. With fruit and vegetables, always look for seasonal produce, as these will be the best quality and price. They should feel firm, as well as appearing smooth and wrinkle-free.

storage guidelines

Keep the more robust fruit and vegetables, such as apples, bananas, potatoes, onions, and garlic, in a cool, dark place but not refrigerated. Store fresh herbs, lettuce, and more delicate items in the crisper drawer of your refrigerator—if you place herbs in a plastic bag with a little splash of water, they will last longer. Mushrooms are best kept in a paper or cloth bag, as they "sweat" in plastic and spoil quickly. Store heavy items on the bottom and more delicate ones on top.

Remove meat, poultry, and seafood from their plastic containers or wrappings, then wash and dry with paper towels and wrap them again loosely in foil. Always store fresh meat and poultry on the bottom shelf of the refrigerator so that no raw juices can drip down onto other foods, and always store cooked meat and poultry away from raw to avoid contamination.

Any fresh meat, poultry, or fish you have left unused can always be frozen. Wrap in foil and place in the freezer or pack in a freezer bag. Ensure frozen food is completely thawed before cooking.

If you store eggs in the refrigerator, remember to remove 1 hour before using to return them to room temperature.

equipment checklist

Your available budget and also how much you cook will to some extent determine what

cooking equipment you buy, but the following is a recommended selection of items. This will ensure that you have everything you need for most dishes and will be a sound investment for the future, especially if you purchase good-quality cookware, which will prove much more durable.

- Selection of 3 saucepans: small, medium, and large
- Large, heavy skillet
- Roasting pan
- Baking sheet
- 3 sharp knives: small, large, and serrated-edged
- Selection of mixing bowls ranging from ramekin size to large
- Measuring cups—plastic is fine
- 2 cutting boards: one for raw foods and the other for everything else
- Large sieve
- Food processor—if you can afford it, this is a great investment and will save you a lot of time.

glossary

Bok choy Chinese greens with delicate dark green leaves and a crunchy white bulb of stalks, available all year round from super-markets. They are high in vitamins, including A and C, as well as calcium, iron, and folic acid.

Chinese five spice powder An aromatic blend of spices used in Asian cooking.

Chorizo A Spanish spiced pork sausage available from the deli section of supermarkets. It has a wonderfully intense savory flavor.

Elderflower cordial A fragrant cordial made from elderflowers and available from most supermarkets.

Frangelico A hazelnut-flavored liqueur produced in Italy, available from larger supermarkets and wine stores or suppliers.

Halloumi cheese A ewes' or goats' milk cheese from Cyprus. It is best cooked—broiled, griddled, fried, or baked—otherwise it can be chewy.

Hokkein noodles Chinese egg noodles, vacuum-packed for freshness and found in the chiller section of larger supermarkets. You can use dried as an alternative, but you will need to double up the quantity given in the recipe.

Jerk seasoning A spice mix used in Caribbean cooking, and available in the spice section of supermarkets and from speciality food stores and suppliers.

Kaffir lime leaves Another Asian ingredient, these leaves have a fantastic lime fragrance and are available from larger supermarkets and Asian markets. Unused leaves freeze well, packed in sealed bags.

Mascarpone cheese A full-fat cream cheese used in Italian cuisine, this is especially useful in cooking, because it never curdles when heated and adds a richness to any dish.

Mirin A rice wine seasoning used in Japanese cooking, available from the Asian section of most supermarkets and health-food stores.

Puy lentils Tiny green lentils with blue veining from France, widely available from supermarkets and health-food stores. Unlike dried beans, lentils don't need presoaking.

Star anise One of the spices used to make Chinese five spice powder, but it is also worth buying the whole spice to flavor Asian dishes.

Sumac A Middle Eastern spice, usually found in its deep red/purple ground form, with a fragrant lemon flavor. It is available from the spice section of larger supermarkets and from speciality food stores and suppliers.

Thai basil leaves A must for achieving an essential Thai flavor, but ordinary basil will do. It is available from some supermarkets and Asian markets.

breakfasts & brunch

bacon & maple syrup pancakes

Serves **4**
Preparation time **5 minutes**
Cooking time **15 minutes**

2½ cups **all-purpose flour**
2½ teaspoons **baking powder**
½ teaspoon **salt**
1 **egg**, lightly beaten
1¾ cups **milk**
2 tablespoons **butter**, melted
spray olive oil, for oiling
8 **slices bacon**
maple syrup, to serve

Sift the flour, baking powder, and salt into a bowl. Make a well in the center and gradually beat in the egg and milk. Continue to beat until the batter is smooth. Stir in the melted butter.

Heat a heavy skillet until hot, spray lightly with spray oil and spoon on about 6 tablespoons of the pancake batter. Cook over a medium heat for 1–2 minutes until bubbles start appearing on the surface. Carefully flip the pancake over and cook for an additional 1–2 minutes until browned on the underside. Remove from the pan and keep warm in a preheated oven, 300°F, while you cook the remainder of the batter—it should make 8 pancakes in total.

Meanwhile, cook the bacon under a preheated high broiler for 2 minutes on each side until golden.

Serve the pancakes topped with the bacon and drizzled with maple syrup.

For pancakes with mixed berries, prepare the pancake batter and cook the pancakes as above. Meanwhile, combine 1½ cups mixed berries with 2 tablespoons confectioners' sugar in a saucepan and warm through over a low heat for 2–3 minutes until soft and juicy. Serve the pancakes topped with the berry sauce and some Greek or whole milk yogurt.

smoked salmon scrambled eggs

Serves **1**
Preparation time **10 minutes**
Cooking time **3–4 minutes**

1 tablespoon **butter**
3 large **eggs**
1 tablespoon **milk**
1 tablespoon **light cream**
  (optional)
1–1½ oz **smoked salmon**,
  cut into narrow strips
1 teaspoon finely snipped
  chives
1–2 slices of hot buttered
  toast
salt and **black pepper**

Melt the butter in a saucepan over a gentle heat until foaming.

Put the eggs in a bowl and mix well with a fork. Add the milk and season with salt and pepper.

Pour the eggs into the foaming butter and cook, stirring constantly with a wooden spoon, scraping the bottom of the pan and bringing the eggs from the outside to the center. The eggs are done when they form soft, creamy curds and are barely set.

Remove the pan from the heat and stir in the cream, if using, salmon, and chives. Pile onto the hot toast on a warmed serving plate. Serve immediately.

For scrambled eggs with goat cheese & herbs, cook the scrambled eggs as above. Once barely set, remove the pan from the heat and stir in 4 oz soft goat cheese and 2 tablespoons chopped mixed herbs. Pile onto the hot toast and serve.

rösti with ham & eggs

Serves **2**
Preparation time **10 minutes**
Cooking time **10–12 minutes**

1 lb **waxy potatoes**, such as
  round red, peeled
2 tablespoons **butter**
2 **eggs**
2 slices of **smoked ham**
salt and **black pepper**
tomato ketchup, to serve

Grate the potatoes using a box grater and place
on a clean dish towel. Wrapping them in the towel,
squeeze out all the excess moisture, transfer to a bowl,
and season to taste with salt and pepper.

Melt the butter in a large nonstick skillet. Divide the
potato mixture into quarters and form each into
a 4 inch cake. Add to the pan and cook over a medium
heat for 5–6 minutes on each side until lightly golden.

Meanwhile, poach or fry the eggs.

Serve 2 röstis per person, topped with an egg and with
a slice of smoked ham and some tomato ketchup.

For sweet potato rösti with egg & spinach, grate
8 oz sweet potato and 8 oz waxy potato and mix
together. Make and cook the rösti as above. Serve 2
röstis topped with a poached egg and a small handful
of baby spinach leaves.

asparagus with frazzled eggs

Serves **4**
Preparation time **10 minutes**
Cooking time **10 minutes**

1 lb **asparagus spears**,
  trimmed
olive oil, for coating and
  pan-frying
4 **eggs**, chilled
salt and **black pepper**
Parmesan shavings, to serve

Blanch the asparagus in a saucepan of salted boiling water for 2 minutes. Drain and refresh under cold water. Drain again, pat dry, and toss in a little oil to coat.

Cook the asparagus in a preheated griddle pan or on a preheated barbecue for 2–3 minutes on each side until tender but still with a bite. Set aside to cool slightly.

Pour enough oil into a large skillet to coat the base generously and heat until almost smoking. Crack each egg into a cup and carefully slide into the pan (watch out as the oil will splutter). Once the edges of the eggs have bubbled up and browned, reduce the heat to low, cover, and cook for 1 minute more. Remove from the pan with a slotted spoon and drain on paper towels. The yolks should have formed a skin, but should remain runny underneath.

Divide the asparagus between 4 warmed plates and top each pile with an egg. Sprinkle with pepper and Parmesan shavings. Serve with a little pot of salt for the eggs.

For soft-cooked eggs with asaparagus & prosciutto "soldiers," blanch 20 asparagus spears as above. Drain and refresh under cold water. Drain again and pat dry. Cut 4 slices of prosciutto into 5 long, thin strips each and wrap each asparagus spear in a strip of ham. Boil 4 eggs in a saucepan of gently simmering water for 4 minutes. Transfer to egg cups, cut off the tops, and serve with the ham-wrapped asparagus spears for dunking.

cheesy turkey & cranberry melt

Serves **4**
Preparation time **5 minutes**
Cooking time **8 minutes**

4 **flat rolls**
2 tablespoons **wholegrain mustard**
2 tablespoons **cranberry sauce**
7 oz **cooked turkey breast,** sliced
1 cup **grated cheddar cheese**

Split the rolls in half and spread half with the mustard and the other half with the cranberry sauce. Top with the turkey slices and cheese and sandwich together.

Heat a dry skillet until hot, add the sandwich, and cook over a medium-high heat for 4 minutes on each side until golden and the cheese has melted. Serve hot.

For avocado, blue cheese, & spinach melt, split the rolls in half and spread the base of each one with a little butter. Mash together 1 peeled, pitted, and sliced avocado, 2 oz crumbled blue cheese and 2 tablespoons heavy cream. Divide between the roll bases and add a few baby spinach leaves. Add the roll tops and cook as above until the filling starts to ooze.

egg & manchego tortillas

Serves **4**
Preparation time **15 minutes**,
  plus cooling
Cooking time **20 minutes**

1 **onion**, finely chopped
1 **green chili**, seeded and
  finely chopped, plus extra
  to serve
1 **corn ear**, kernels removed,
  or 4 tablespoons **canned
  corn**
10 **eggs**, beaten
2 tablespoons **butter**
3 oz **Manchego cheese**,
  crumbled, plus extra
  shavings to serve
1 tablespoon **cilantro**,
  chopped, plus extra to serve
8 **flour tortillas**, warmed in
  the oven
salt and **black pepper**
snipped **chives**, to garnish
4 tablespoons **sweet chili
  sauce**

Stir the onion, chili, and corn kernels into the beaten eggs in a bowl. Season well with salt and pepper.

Melt the butter in a large saucepan until foaming. Add the egg mixture and cook over a medium heat, stirring constantly, until the eggs are softly scrambled. Immediately remove the pan from the heat and stir in the crumbled Manchego and cilantro.

Serve immediately on the warmed tortillas sprinkled with green chili slices, fresh cilantro, and chives, plus shavings of Manchego and the sweet chili sauce.

For homemade guacamole to serve with the tortillas in place of the sweet chili sauce, put 1 peeled, pitted, and diced avocado in a food processor or blender with 1 crushed garlic clove, 1 seeded and chopped red chili, juice of 1 lime, 1 tablespoon chopped fresh cilantro, and salt and pepper to taste. Process until fairly smooth and transfer to a bowl. Stir in 1 seeded and finely chopped tomato.

bacon & egg crispy bread tarts

Serves **4**
Preparation time **10 minutes**
Cooking time **35 minutes**

spray olive oil, for oiling
16 slices of **white bread**
⅓ cup **butter**, melted
5 oz **bacon slices**, rind
  removed, diced
2 **eggs**
½ cup **heavy cream**
2 tablespoons freshly grated
  Parmesan cheese
8 **vine cherry tomatoes**
salt and **black pepper**

Spray a muffin pan lightly with spray oil. Cut the crusts off the bread and discard. Flatten each bread slice by rolling over it firmly with a rolling pin. Brush each slice with the melted butter and place 8 of the slices diagonally on top of the others to form the bases. Carefully press each base into a cup of the prepared muffin pan, making sure that they fit evenly (they need to reach up the sides).

Bake in a preheated oven, 400°F, for 12–15 minutes until crisp and golden.

Meanwhile, heat a dry skillet until hot, add the bacon, and cook for 2–3 minutes until crisp and golden.

Divide the bacon between the baked bread shells. Beat together the eggs, cream, cheese, and salt and pepper to taste in a bowl. Spoon into the cases and top each with a cherry tomato. Bake in the oven for 15 minutes until set.

For spinach & egg tarts, prepare and bake the bread shells as above. Meanwhile, melt 1 tablespoon butter in a skillet, add 2½ cups baby spinach leaves, and cook gently for 2–3 minutes until just wilted. Drain well and dry on paper towels. Divide the spinach between the bread shells. Beat together the eggs, cream, cheese, and salt and pepper to taste as above and pour over the spinach. Bake in the oven for 15 minutes until set.

freeform spinach, feta, & egg tarts

Serves **4**
Preparation time **15 minutes**
Cooking time **20 minutes**

1 cup **frozen leaf spinach**,
   thawed
4 oz **feta cheese**, diced
2 tablespoons **mascarpone
   cheese**
pinch of freshly grated
   nutmeg
4 sheets of **phyllo pastry**,
   thawed if frozen
¼ cup **butter**, melted
4 **eggs**
salt and **black pepper**

Drain the spinach and squeeze out all the excess water, then chop finely. Put in a bowl and mix in the feta, mascarpone, nutmeg, and salt and pepper to taste.

Lay the sheets of phyllo pastry on top of one another, brushing each with a little melted butter. Cut out four 6 inch rounds using a saucer as a template.

Divide the spinach mixture between the pastry rounds, spreading the filling out but leaving a 1 inch border. Gather the edges up and over the filling to form a rim. Make a shallow well in the spinach mixture.

Transfer the tarts to a baking sheet and bake in a preheated oven, 400°F, for 8 minutes.

Remove from the oven and carefully crack an egg into each hollow. Return to the oven and bake for an additional 8–10 minutes until the eggs are set.

For spinach & goat cheese parcels, prepare the spinach as above, then mix with 4 oz soft goat cheese, 2 tablespoons mascarpone cheese, a pinch of ground cumin, and salt and pepper to taste. Cut out the phyllo pastry rounds as above and divide the spinach mixture between them, but place it on one half of each round. Carefully fold the pastry over the filling and turn the pastry edges over to seal. Bake in the oven as above and serve with lemon wedges for squeezing over and Greek or whole milk yogurt.

eggs benedict

Serves **4**
Preparation time **5 minutes**
Cooking time **15 minutes**

8 thick slices of **cooked ham**
4 **muffins** or **brioche**
2 tablespoons **butter**
8 hot **poached eggs**
snipped **chives**, to garnish

Hollandaise sauce
3 **egg yolks**
1 tablespoon **cold water**
½ cup **butter**, softened
large pinch of **salt**
2 pinches of **cayenne**
   pepper
1 teaspoon **lemon juice**
1 tablespoon **light cream**

Warm the ham slices under a preheated high broiler for 2–3 minutes on each side. Transfer to an ovenproof dish and keep warm in a low oven.

Make the sauce. Beat the egg yolks and measurement water together in the top of a double boiler over simmering water until the mixture is pale. Gradually add the butter, a small amount at a time, and continue beating until the mixture thickens. Add the salt, 1 pinch of cayenne pepper, and lemon juice. Stir in the cream. Remove from the heat and keep warm.

Split the muffins or brioche in half, then toast and spread with the butter. Arrange on warmed plates. Lay a slice of ham on each muffin half and top with a poached egg. Spoon a little of the sauce over each egg. Garnish with the remaining cayenne pepper and chives and serve immediately.

summer berry granola

Serves **4**
Preparation time **10 minutes**
Cooking time **8–9 minutes**

spray olive oil, for oiling
2 cups **rolled oats**
⅔ cup toasted and roughly
  chopped **mixed nuts**
1 tablespoon **maple syrup**,
  plus extra to serve
1¼ cups **milk**, plus extra to
  serve
1 cup **mixed summer
  berries**
Greek or **whole milk yogurt**,
  to serve

Spray a baking sheet lightly with spray oil. Put the oats and nuts in a bowl and stir in the maple syrup. Spread the mixture out on the prepared baking sheet and bake in a preheated oven, 350°F, for 5 minutes.

Remove from the oven and stir well. Return to the oven and bake for an additional 3–4 minutes until lightly toasted. Allow to cool.

Divide the granola between 4 serving bowls and pour over the milk. Add the berries and serve with yogurt and a drizzle of maple syrup.

For Bircher muesli, put the oats and nuts in a bowl and stir in the maple syrup as above, then add 2½ cups milk to the oat mixture. Allow to soak for at least 2 hours (or even overnight in the refrigerator) and serve topped with fruits of your choice and plain yogurt.

broiled peaches with passion fruit

Serves **4**
Preparation time **2 minutes**
Cooking time **4–5 minutes**

6 large ripe **peaches**
2 tablespoons **honey**, plus
   extra to serve
2 teaspoons **ground**
   cinnamon

To serve
½ cup **Greek** or **whole milk**
   yogurt
pulp from 2 **passion fruit**

Cut the peaches in half and discard the pits. Arrange the peach halves cut side up in a foil-lined broiler pan, drizzle over the honey, and dust with the cinnamon.

Cook under a preheated high broiler for 4–5 minutes until lightly charred.

Spoon into serving bowls and serve each one topped with yogurt, an extra drizzle of honey, and the passion fruit pulp.

For broiled figs with maple syrup & pecans, cut 6 large ripe figs in half and drizzle over 2 tablespoons maple syrup. Cook under a preheated high broiler for 2–3 minutes until softened. Transfer to serving plates and top each with a spoonful of crème fraîche or whole milk yogurt, a few toasted chopped pecan nuts, and an extra drizzle of maple syrup.

chili chocolate chip muffins

Makes **8**
Preparation time **10 minutes**
Cooking time **20 minutes**

1¾ cups **self-rising flour**
½ cup **cocoa powder**
1 teaspoon **baking powder**
⅔ cup **light brown sugar**
1 **egg**, lightly beaten
1 cup **milk**
¼ cup **butter**, melted
½ cup **chili chocolate** or
   bittersweet chocolate,
   chopped, and a pinch of
   chili powder
¾ cup **pecan nuts**, toasted
   and roughly ground
spray olive oil, for oiling

Cut a 6 inch square from parchment paper and use it as a template to cut 7 more. Fold them all into quarters. Open out flat and set aside.

Sift the flour, cocoa powder, and baking powder into a bowl and stir in the sugar. Beat together the egg, milk, and melted butter in a small bowl, then mix into the dry ingredients until just combined (don't overmix). Fold in the chocolate and pecan nuts.

Spray each square of parchment paper with spray oil and press each piece into the cup of a muffin pan. Spoon the chocolate mixture into the lined holes and bake in a preheated oven, 400°F, for 20 minutes until risen and golden. Allow to cool slightly on a cooling rack and serve warm.

For white chocolate & raspberry muffins, sift 2 cups self-rising flour and 1 teaspoon baking powder into a bowl and stir in ⅔ cup light brown sugar. Beat together 1 lightly beaten egg, 1 cup milk, and ¼ cup melted butter, then mix into the dry ingredients until just combined (don't overmix). Fold in ½ cup chopped white chocolate and 1 cup small raspberries. Bake in the oven as above and serve warm.

soups &
one-pot
meals

pork chops baked with potatoes

Serves **4**
Preparation time **10 minutes**
Cooking time **45–50 minutes**

1 ½ lb **potatoes**, peeled
2 tablespoons **extra virgin
    olive oil**
4 large **pork chops**, about
    8 oz each
4 oz **piece of smoked bacon**,
    rind removed, diced
1 large **onion**, sliced
2 **garlic cloves**, chopped
2 teaspoons **dried oregano**
grated **zest** and **juice** of
    1 **lemon**
1 cup **chicken stock** (see
    page 44 for homemade)
salt and **black pepper**
a few **thyme leaves**, to
    garnish (optional)

Cut the potatoes into 1 inch cubes. Heat the oil in an
ovenproof skillet or flameproof casserole, add the pork
chops, and cook over a high heat for 1–2 minutes on
each side until browned. Remove from the pan with a
slotted spoon.

Reduce the heat to medium, add the bacon and onion,
and cook, stirring, for 3–4 minutes until golden. Add the
potatoes, garlic, oregano, and lemon zest and stir well.
Pour in the stock and lemon juice and season lightly
with salt and pepper.

Transfer to a preheated oven, 350°F, and bake,
uncovered, for 20 minutes. Arrange the chops on top
and bake for an additional 20 minutes until the potatoes
and pork are cooked through.

For pork chops with roasted sweet potatoes & sage,
use 1 ½ lb sweet potatoes, peeled and cut into cubes,
instead of the potatoes and cook as above. Continue
with the recipe, but use 1 tablespoon chopped sage in
place of the dried oregano.

chicken, vegetable, & lentil stew

Serves **6**
Preparation time **15 minutes**
Cooking time **2 hours**

2 lb **skinless chicken thigh
    fillets**, halved
2 tablespoons **all-purpose
    flour**, seasoned with salt
    and black pepper
3 tablespoons **olive oil**
1 large **onion**, chopped
2 **carrots**, chopped
2 **celery sticks**, chopped
2 **garlic cloves**, crushed
⅔ cup **dry white wine**
4 cups **chicken stock** (see
    below for homemade)
1 tablespoon chopped
    rosemary
¾ cup **Puy lentils**
salt and **black pepper**

Dust the chicken thighs with the seasoned flour to coat lightly.

Heat half the oil in a flameproof casserole, add the chicken, in 2 batches, and cook over a medium-high heat for 5 minutes until browned on both sides. Remove from the pan with a slotted spoon.

Reduce the heat to medium and add the remaining oil to the pan. Add the onion, carrots, celery, garlic, and salt and pepper to taste and cook, stirring frequently, for 5 minutes. Add the wine, stock, rosemary, and lentils and return the chicken thighs to the pan.

Bring to a boil, stirring, then reduce the heat, cover, and simmer gently for 1½ hours until the vegetables and lentils are tender.

For homemade chicken stock, chop a cooked chicken carcass into 3–4 pieces and put in a large saucepan with any trimmings from the chicken, 1 roughly chopped onion, 2 roughly chopped large carrots, 1 roughly chopped large celery stick, 1 bay leaf, a few lightly crushed parsley stalks, 1 thyme sprig, and 7 cups cold water. Bring to a boil, skimming off any scum that rises to the surface. Reduce the heat and simmer, uncovered, for 2 hours. Strain through a fine sieve and allow to cool completely before refrigerating. When chilled, remove any solidified fat from the surface. This makes about 4 cups of stock.

baked cod with tomatoes & olives

Serves **4**
Preparation time **5 minutes**
Cooking time **15 minutes**

8 oz **cherry tomatoes**, halved
½ cup **pitted black olives**
2 tablespoons **capers in brine**, drained
4 **thyme sprigs**, plus extra for garnish
4 **cod fillets**, about 6 oz each
2 tablespoons **extra virgin olive oil**
2 tablespoons **balsamic vinegar**
salt and **black pepper**

Combine the tomatoes, olives, capers, and thyme sprigs in a roasting pan. Nestle the cod fillets in the pan, drizzle over the oil and balsamic vinegar, and season to taste with salt and pepper.

Bake in a preheated oven, 400°F, for 15 minutes.

Transfer the fish, tomatoes, and olives to warmed plates. Spoon the pan juices over the fish. Serve immediately with a mixed green leaf salad.

For steamed cod with lemon, arrange a cod fillet on each of 4 x 12 inch squares of foil. Top each with ½ teaspoon grated lemon zest, a squeeze of lemon juice, 1 tablespoon extra virgin olive oil, and salt and pepper to taste. Seal the edges of the foil together to form parcels, transfer to a baking sheet, and cook in a preheated oven, 400°F, for 15 minutes. Remove and allow to rest for 5 minutes. Open the parcels and serve sprinkled with chopped parsley.

beef goulash

Serves **8**
Preparation time **10 minutes**
Cooking time **2–2½ hours**

4 tablespoons **olive oil**
3 lb **braising steak**, cubed
2 **onions**, sliced
2 **red bell peppers**, cored,
    seeded, and diced
1 tablespoon **smoked
    paprika**
2 tablespoons chopped
    marjoram
1 teaspoon **caraway seeds**
4 cups **beef stock** (see
    below for homemade)
5 tablespoons **tomato paste**
salt and **black pepper**

Heat the oil in a flameproof casserole, add the beef, in 3 batches, and cook over a high heat for 5 minutes until browned all over. Remove from the pan with a slotted spoon.

Add the onions and red peppers to the pan and cook gently for 10 minutes until softened. Stir in the paprika, marjoram, and caraway seeds and cook, stirring, for 1 minute more.

Return the beef to the pan, add the stock, tomato paste, and salt and pepper to taste and bring to a boil, stirring. Reduce the heat, cover, and simmer gently for 1½–2 hours. You can remove the lid for the final 30 minutes if the sauce needs thickening.

For homemade beef stock, put 1½ lb cubed beef shank, 2 chopped onions, 2–3 chopped carrots, 2 roughly chopped celery sticks, 1 bay leaf, 1 bouquet garni, 4–6 black peppercorns, and 7 cups cold water in a large saucepan. Slowly bring to a boil, then reduce the heat, cover with a well-fitting lid, and simmer gently for 2 hours, skimming off any scum that rises to the surface. Strain through a fine sieve and allow to cool before refrigerating. This makes about 6 cups of stock.

molasses & mustard beans

Serves **6**
Preparation time **10 minutes**
Cooking time **1 hour 35 minutes**

1 **carrot**, diced
1 **celery stick**, chopped
1 **onion**, chopped
2 **garlic cloves**, crushed
2 x 13 oz cans **soy beans**, drained
3 cups **passata (sieved tomatoes)**
3 oz **bacon slices**, diced
2 tablespoons **molasses**
2 teaspoons **Dijon mustard**
salt and **black pepper**

Put all the ingredients in a flameproof casserole and bring slowly to a boil, stirring occasionally.

Cover, transfer to a preheated oven, 325°F, and bake for 1 hour.

Remove the lid and bake for an additional 30 minutes. Serve with garlic-rubbed bread (see below).

For garlic-rubbed bread to serve with the beans, heat a ridged griddle pan until hot, add 6 thick slices of sourdough bread and cook for 2 minutes on each side until lightly charred. Rub each bread slice with a peeled garlic clove (or 2) and drizzle with extra virgin olive oil.

beef, pickled onion, & beer stew

Serves **4**
Preparation time **10 minutes**
Cooking time **2¼ hours**

2 lb **braising steak**, cubed
3 tablespoons **all-purpose flour**, seasoned with salt and black pepper
2 tablespoons **olive oil**
1 lb jar **pickled onions**, drained
2 **carrots**, thickly sliced
1¼ cups **English beer**
2½ cups **beef stock** (see page 48 for homemade)
4 tablespoons **tomato paste**
1 tablespoon **Worcestershire sauce**
2 **bay leaves**
salt and **black pepper**
few sprigs fresh **parsley**, chopped, to garnish

Dust the beef with the seasoned flour to coat lightly.

Heat the oil in a large flameproof casserole, add the beef, in 3 batches, and cook over a high heat for 5 minutes until browned all over, removing from the pan with a slotted spoon. Return all the beef to the pan.

Add the onions and carrots to the pan and stir well, then gradually stir in the beer and stock and bring to a boil. Stir in the tomato paste, Worcestershire sauce, bay leaves, and salt and pepper to taste.

Cover, transfer to a preheated oven, 325°F, and cook for 2 hours, stirring halfway through, until the beef and vegetables are tender. Garnish with the parsley and serve with soft polenta (see below).

For soft polenta to serve with the stew, bring 4 cups water to a rolling boil in a saucepan, add 2 teaspoons salt and gradually beat in 1 cup cornmeal, stirring constantly until the mixture boils. Cook for 5 minutes, remove from the heat, and stir in ¼ cup butter and 4 tablespoons freshly grated Parmesan cheese. Add salt and pepper to taste.

chicken & rice bake

Serves **4**
Preparation time **15 minutes**
Cooking time **1 hour**

8 skinless **chicken thigh
   fillets**, about 1½ lb in total
8 **bacon slices**, rind removed
2 tablespoons **olive oil**
1¼ cups **long-grain rice**
1 **onion**, chopped
2 **garlic cloves**, crushed
1 teaspoon **ground turmeric**
grated **zest** and **juice** of
   ½ **lemon**
2 cups hot **chicken stock**
   (see page 44 for
   homemade)
1 tablespoon chopped
   cilantro
salt and **black pepper**

Wrap each chicken thigh with a bacon slice and secure in place with a toothpick.

Heat the oil in a flameproof casserole, add the chicken, and cook over a high heat for 5 minutes until browned all over. Remove with a slotted spoon.

Add the rice to the pan and cook over a low heat, stirring, for 1 minute. Add the onion, garlic, turmeric, lemon zest, stock, and salt and pepper to taste. Arrange the chicken thighs over the rice, pressing down gently.

Cover with a layer of foil, then the lid. Transfer to a preheated oven, 350°F, and bake for 50 minutes.

Remove from the oven and stir in the cilantro and lemon juice. Discard the toothpicks and serve with a tangy yogurt sauce (see below).

For tangy yogurt sauce to serve with the rice, combine ⅔ cup Greek or whole milk yogurt with 1 teaspoon grated lemon zest, 1 crushed garlic clove, 2 teaspoons lemon juice, 1 tablespoon chopped parsley, and salt and pepper to taste in a bowl.

pumpkin soup with crispy bacon

Serves **4**
Preparation time **10 minutes**
Cooking time **30 minutes**

2 lb **pumpkin**, peeled and
    seeded
2 tablespoons **extra virgin**
    olive oil
1 large **onion**, sliced
2 **garlic cloves**, crushed
½ teaspoon **smoked paprika**
5 cups **chicken stock** (see
    page 44 for homemade)
4 **bacon slices**, rind removed
salt and **black pepper**

Cut the pumpkin into 1 inch cubes and put in a roasting pan. Add 1 tablespoon olive oil and stir well. Roast in a preheated oven, 400°F, for 25 minutes.

Meanwhile, heat 1 tablespoon olive oil in a large saucepan, add the onion, garlic, paprika, and a little salt and pepper and cook gently for 10 minutes until soft.

Add the cooked pumpkin and stock to the pan, bring to a boil, and cook for 5 minutes. Transfer to a food processor or blender and process until smooth.

Meanwhile, cook the bacon under a preheated high broiler until crisp.

Spoon the soup into warmed bowls. Break the bacon into small pieces and sprinkle on top, and drizzle the remaining oil over the soup.

For pumpkin soup with olive salsa, combine ⅔ cup pitted black olives, chopped, 2 tablespoons extra virgin olive oil, grated zest of ½ lemon, 1 tablespoon chopped parsley, and pepper to taste in a bowl. Make the pumpkin soup as above and serve topped with the olive salsa.

garlic, paprika, & egg soup

Serves **4**

Preparation time **10 minutes**

Cooking time **20 minutes**

4 tablespoons **olive oil**

12 thick slices of **baguette**

5 **garlic cloves**, sliced

1 **onion**, finely chopped

1 tablespoon **paprika**

1 teaspoon **ground cumin**

good pinch of **saffron threads**

5 cups **vegetable stock** (see below for homemade)

1 oz **dried soup pasta**

4 **eggs**

salt and **black pepper**

Heat the oil in a heavy saucepan, add the bread slices, and cook gently, turning once, until golden. Remove from the pan with a slotted spoon and drain on paper towels.

Add the garlic, onion, paprika, and cumin to the pan and cook gently, stirring, for 3 minutes. Add the saffron and stock and bring to a boil. Stir in the soup pasta. Reduce the heat, cover, and simmer for about 8 minutes, or until the pasta is just tender. Season to taste with salt and pepper.

Break the eggs onto a saucer and slide into the pan, one at a time. Cook for about 2 minutes, or until poached.

Stack 3 fried bread slices in each of 4 warmed soup bowls. Ladle the soup over the bread, making sure that each serving contains an egg. Serve immediately.

For homemade vegetable stock, put 1¼ lb mixed vegetables, such as carrots, leeks, celery, onions, and mushrooms, chopped, 1 garlic clove, peeled but left whole, 8 black peppercorns, 1 bouquet garni, and 6 cups cold water in a large saucepan. Bring to a boil, then reduce the heat and simmer gently, uncovered, for 30 minutes, skimming off any scum that rises to the surface. Strain the stock through a fine sieve and allow to cool completely before refrigerating. This will make around 5 cups of stock.

chicken noodle soup

Serves **4**

Preparation time **10 minutes**, plus cooling

Cooking time **40 minutes**

2 **chicken quarters**, about 1½ lb in total

1 **onion**, chopped

4 **garlic cloves**, chopped

3 slices of **fresh ginger root**, peeled and bruised

8 cups **cold water**

4 oz **dried egg thread noodles**

2 tablespoons **light soy sauce**

1 **red bird's eye chili**, seeded and sliced

2 **scallions**, sliced

2 tablespoons **cilantro leaves**

salt and **black pepper**

Put the chicken quarters, onion, garlic, ginger, measurement water, and salt and pepper to taste in a saucepan. Bring to a boil, then reduce the heat and simmer gently, uncovered, for 30 minutes, skimming off any scum that rises to the surface.

Remove the chicken and strain the stock. Allow to cool, and meanwhile skin the chicken and shred the flesh.

Cook the noodles in boiling water for 6 minutes. Drain well and divide between 4 bowls.

Heat the stock in a saucepan with the soy sauce. Add the chicken and simmer for 5 minutes.

Spoon the stock and chicken over the noodles and sprinkle with the chili, scallion slices, and cilantro leaves. Serve immediately.

For Thai chicken noodle soup, cook the chicken quarters with the other ingredients in the water as above, adding 6 large torn kaffir lime leaves. Remove the chicken and strain the stock. When cool, skin the chicken and shred as above. Heat the stock in a saucepan with 2 tablespoons Thai fish sauce, juice of ½ lime, 2 teaspoons superfine sugar and 1 seeded and sliced red bird's eye chili. Add the chicken and simmer for 5 minutes. Meanwhile, put 4 oz dried rice noodles in a large heatproof bowl, pour over enough boiling water to cover, and let stand for 5 minutes until just tender, then drain. Serve the noodles with the stock and chicken spooned over, garnished with sliced chilies, cilantro leaves, and shredded kaffir lime leaves.

gazpacho

Serves **4**
Preparation time **10 minutes**,
  plus chilling
Cooking time **25 minutes**

1½ lb ripe **tomatoes**
1 large **fennel bulb**
1¼ cups **salted boiling water**
¾ teaspoon **coriander seeds**
½ teaspoon **mixed
  peppercorns**
1 tablespoon **extra virgin
  olive oil**
1 large **garlic clove**, crushed
1 small **onion**, chopped
1 tablespoon **balsamic
  vinegar**
1 tablespoon **lemon juice**
¾ teaspoon chopped
  oregano, plus extra leaves
  to garnish
1 teaspoon **tomato paste**
1 rounded teaspoon **rock
  salt**
green olives, finely sliced, to
  garnish

Put the tomatoes in a large saucepan or heatproof bowl and pour over enough boiling water to cover, then leave for about 1 minute. Drain, skin the tomatoes carefully, and roughly chop the flesh.

Trim the green fronds from the fennel and discard. Finely slice the bulb, put in a saucepan, and pour over the measurement salted boiling water. Cover and simmer for 10 minutes.

Meanwhile, crush the coriander seeds and peppercorns in a mortar with a pestle. Heat the oil in a large saucepan, add the crushed spices, garlic, and onion, and cook gently for 5 minutes.

Add the vinegar, lemon juice, tomatoes, and chopped oregano to the onion mixture. Stir well and then add the fennel and its cooking water, the tomato paste, and salt. Bring to a simmer and let cook, uncovered, for 10 minutes.

Transfer to a food processor or blender and process to preferred consistency. Allow to cool, then chill overnight or for at least several hours. Serve garnished with the oregano leaves and olive slices.

For roasted tomato gazpacho place 1½ lb halved tomatoes in a roasting pan with 2 tablespoons extra virgin olive oil and a little salt and pepper to taste. Roast in a preheated oven, 400°F, for 25 minutes until roasted. Allow to cool and then, following the above recipe, process with the remaining ingredients replacing the oregano with 1 tablespoon chopped fresh basil. Chill for 1 hour before serving.

pea, lettuce, & lemon soup

Serves **4**
Preparation time **10 minutes**
Cooking time **20 minutes**

2 tablespoons **butter**
1 large **onion**, finely
  chopped
2¾ cups **frozen peas**
2 small **crisphead lettuces**,
  roughly chopped
4 cups **vegetable** or **chicken
  stock** (see pages 58 and
  44 for homemade)
grated **zest** and **juice** of
  ½ **lemon**
salt and **black pepper**

Sesame croutons
2 thick slices of **multigrain
  bread**, cubed
1 tablespoon **olive oil**
1 tablespoon **sesame seeds**

Make the croutons. Brush the bread cubes with the oil and spread out in a roasting pan. Sprinkle with the sesame seeds and bake in a preheated oven, 400°F, for 10–15 minutes, or until golden.

Meanwhile, melt the butter in a large saucepan, add the onion, and cook gently for 5 minutes, or until softened. Add the peas, lettuce, stock, lemon zest and juice, and salt and pepper to taste. Bring to a boil, then reduce the heat, cover, and simmer for 10–15 minutes.

Allow the soup to cool slightly, then transfer to a food processor or blender and process until smooth. Return the soup to the pan, adjust the seasoning if necessary, and reheat gently. Spoon into warmed serving bowls and sprinkle with the croutons.

For ricotta & mint croutons instead of the sesame croutons, cut 8 thin slices of baguette and lightly toast under a preheated medium broiler for 2 minutes on each side until golden. Rub over each side with a peeled garlic clove and drizzle with 1 tablespoon extra virgin olive oil. Spread the toasts with ½ cup ricotta cheese and arrange 2 on each soup serving. Sprinkle with 2 tablespoons sliced mint leaves, season to taste with salt and pepper, and drizzle with a little extra oil.

chili bean & red pepper soup

Serves **6**
Preparation time **20 minutes**
Cooking time **40 minutes**

2 tablespoons **sunflower oil**
1 large **onion**, finely chopped
4 **garlic cloves**, finely chopped
2 **red bell peppers**, cored, seeded, and diced
2 **red chilies**, seeded and finely chopped
3¾ cups **vegetable stock** (see page 58 for homemade)
3 cups **tomato juice** or **passata (sieved tomatoes)**
2 tablespoons **sweet chili sauce**, or more to taste
13 oz can **red kidney beans**, drained
2 tablespoons finely chopped **cilantro**
salt and **black pepper**
rind of 1 **lime**, cut into strips, to garnish (optional)

To serve
5 tablespoons **sour cream** or **crème fraîche**
tortilla chips

Heat the oil in a large saucepan, add the onion and garlic, and cook gently for 5 minutes, or until softened but not browned. Stir in the red peppers and chilies and cook for a few minutes. Stir in the stock and tomato juice or passata, chili sauce, beans, cilantro, and salt and pepper to taste. Bring to a boil, then reduce the heat, cover, and simmer for 30 minutes.

Allow to cool slightly, then transfer to a food processor or blender and process until smooth. Return the soup to the pan and adjust the seasoning, adding a little extra chili sauce if necessary. Reheat gently.

Spoon into warmed soup bowls. Stir a little sour cream or crème fraîche into each portion and garnish with lime rind strips, if desired. Serve with tortilla chips.

For crispy sliced tortilla wedges to serve with the soup, cut each of 2 large flour tortillas into 12 wedges. Spray with olive oil spray and season with salt, pepper, and a little cayenne pepper. Lay on a broiler rack, spice-side up, and toast under a preheated medium broiler for 1–2 minutes until crisp.

20-minute suppers

pork chops with caramel pears

Serves **4**
Preparation time **5 minutes**
Cooking time **15–20 minutes**

2 **Bartlett pears**, cored and
    thickly sliced
2 tablespoons **light brown
    sugar**
4 **pork chops**, about 8 oz
    each
¼ cup **unsalted butter**
12 large **sage leaves**
1 cup **hot chicken stock** (see
    page 44 for homemade)
salt and **black pepper**

Toss the pear slices with the sugar and set aside.
Season the pork chops with salt and pepper.

Melt half the butter in a skillet, add the sage leaves,
and cook over a high heat for about 3 minutes, or until
crisp. Remove from the pan with a slotted spoon and
set aside.

Add the chops to the pan and cook over a medium
heat for 3–4 minutes on each side, or until golden.
Remove from the pan, cover loosely with foil, and
keep warm.

Melt the remaining butter in the pan, add the pear
slices, and cook for 2 minutes until golden. Remove
from the pan with a slotted spoon and set aside with
the chops.

Pour the stock into the pan and simmer gently for
2–3 minutes, or until reduced and thickened slightly.
Serve the chops and pear slices with the sauce,
garnished with the crispy sage.

For green beans with garlic & lemon to serve as
an accompaniment, blanch 12 oz green beans in a
saucepan of salted boiling water for 2 minutes. Drain
and refresh under cold water. Drain again and pat
dry. Heat 2 tablespoons extra virgin olive oil in a large
skillet, add 2 sliced garlic cloves, and cook gently,
stirring, for 3 minutes until soft. Stir in the beans and a
squeeze of lemon juice and season to taste with salt
and pepper.

asian chicken parcels

Serves **4**
Preparation time **5 minutes**
Cooking time **15 minutes**

4 **skinless chicken breast fillets**, about 8 oz each
5 tablespoons **light soy sauce**
1 tablespoon **honey**
2 **garlic cloves**, sliced
2 **red chilies**, seeded and finely chopped
1 inch piece of **fresh ginger root**, peeled and finely shredded
4 **star anise**
3 **baby bok choy**, quartered

Score each chicken breast several times with a knife and put one on each of 4 x 12 inch squares of foil.

Combine the soy sauce, honey, garlic, chilies, ginger, and star anise in a small bowl, then spoon over the chicken.

Arrange 3 bok choy quarters on top of the chicken breasts. Seal the edges of the foil together to form parcels, transfer to a baking sheet, and bake in a preheated oven, 400°F, for 15 minutes until the chicken is cooked through.

Allow to rest for 5 minutes, then serve the parcels with boiled jasmine rice.

For Mediterranean chicken parcels, score the chicken breasts as above, put on the foil squares, and season with salt and pepper. Top with 2 teaspoons dried oregano, 2 chopped tomatoes, ⅓ cup pitted black olives, chopped, 2 tablespoons drained capers in brine, and a good drizzle of extra virgin olive oil. Cook in the oven as above and serve with a mixed leaf salad and some crusty bread.

vegetable & tofu stir-fry

Serves **4**
Preparation time **10 minutes**
Cooking time **7 minutes**

3 tablespoons **sunflower oil**
10 oz **firm tofu**, cubed
1 **onion**, sliced
2 **carrots**, sliced
5 oz **broccoli**, broken into
   small florets and stalks
   sliced
1 **red bell pepper**, cored,
   seeded, and sliced
1 large **zucchini**, sliced
5 oz **sugar snap peas**
2 tablespoons **soy sauce**
2 tablespoons **sweet chili
   sauce**
½ cup **water**

To garnish
chopped **red chilies**
Thai or **ordinary basil leaves**

Heat 1 tablespoon of the oil in a wok or large skillet until starting to smoke, add the tofu, and stir-fry over a high heat for 2 minutes until golden. Remove from the pan with a slotted spoon.

Heat the remaining oil in the pan, add the onion and carrots, and stir-fry for 1½ minutes. Add the broccoli and red pepper and stir-fry for 1 minute, then add the zucchini and sugar snap peas and stir-fry for 1 minute.

Combine the soy and chili sauces and measurement water and add to the pan with the tofu. Cook for 1 minute. Serve in bowls, garnished with chopped red chilies and basil leaves.

For sesame noodles to serve as an accompaniment, put 12 oz egg thread noodles in a large heatproof bowl, pour over enough boiling water to cover, and allow to stand for 4 minutes until just tender. Drain well, then toss with 1 tablespoon light soy sauce and 2 teaspoons sesame oil. Serve sprinkled with 1 tablespoon toasted sesame seeds.

asian tuna salad

Serves **4**

Preparation time **10 minutes**, plus marinating

Cooking time **1 minute**

12 oz **fresh tuna steak**, cut into strips

3 tablespoons **soy sauce**

1 teaspoon **wasabi paste**

1 tablespoon **sake** or **dry white wine**

4 cups **mixed salad leaves**

5 oz **baby yellow tomatoes**, halved

1 **cucumber**, sliced into wide fine strips

Dressing

2 tablespoons **soy sauce**

1 tablespoon **lime juice**

1 teaspoon **brown sugar**

2 teaspoons **sesame oil**

Combine the tuna with the soy sauce, wasabi, and sake or wine in a bowl. Cover and allow to marinate for 10 minutes.

Arrange the salad leaves, tomatoes, and cucumber on serving plates.

Make the dressing. Put all the ingredients in a bowl and beat together with a fork or put in a screw-top jar and shake to combine.

Heat a dry nonstick pan over a high heat, add the tuna, and cook for about 10 seconds on each side or until seared. Place the tuna on top of the salad, drizzle with the dressing, and serve.

For Thai tuna salad, leave the tuna steak whole and omit the marinating. Heat a ridged griddle pan until very hot, add the tuna, and cook over a high heat for 30 seconds on each side. Remove from the pan and allow to rest briefly. Meanwhile, beat together 1 tablespoon Thai fish sauce, 1 tablespoon lime juice, and 2 teaspoons superfine sugar in a bowl, then add 1 finely sliced red chili and 1 crushed garlic clove. Slice the tuna thinly and arrange over the salad leaves, tomatoes, and cucumber on serving plates as above. Drizzle over the dressing and serve.

thai chicken curry

Serves **4**
Preparation time **5 minutes**
Cooking time **15 minutes**

1 tablespoon **sunflower oil**
1 tablespoon **Thai green curry paste** (see below for homemade)
6 **kaffir lime leaves**, torn
2 tablespoons **Thai fish sauce**
1 tablespoon **light brown sugar**
¾ cup **chicken stock**
1⅔ cups **coconut milk**
1 lb **skinless chicken thigh fillets**, diced
4 oz can **bamboo shoots**, drained
4 oz can **baby corn**
1 large handful **Thai basil leaves** or **cilantro leaves**, plus extra to garnish
1 tablespoon **lime juice**
1 **red chili**, sliced, to garnish

Heat the oil in a wok or large skillet, add the curry paste and lime leaves, and stir-fry over a low heat for 1–2 minutes until fragrant.

Add the fish sauce, sugar, stock, and coconut milk and bring to a boil, then reduce the heat and simmer gently for 5 minutes.

Add the chicken and cook for 5 minutes. Add the bamboo shoots and baby corn and cook for an additional 3 minutes.

Stir through the basil or cilantro leaves and lime juice, then serve garnished with the leaves and chili.

For homemade Thai green curry paste, put 15 small green chilies, 4 halved garlic cloves, 2 finely chopped lemon grass stalks, 2 torn Kaffir lime leaves, 2 chopped shallots, 1 inch piece of peeled and finely chopped fresh ginger root, 2 teaspoons black peppercorns, 1 teaspoon pared lime rind, ½ teaspoon salt, and 1 tablespoon peanut oil in a food processor or blender and process to a thick paste. Transfer to a screw-top jar. This makes about ⅔ cup of paste, which can be stored in the refrigerator for up to 3 weeks.

seared beef & broccoli bruschetta

Serves **4**
Preparation time **5 minutes**
Cooking time **10 minutes**

1½ cups **broccoli florets**
1 lb **sirloin steak**
5 tablespoons **extra virgin olive oil**
4 slices of **sourdough bread**
2 **garlic cloves**, sliced
1 small **red chili**, seeded and finely chopped
1 tablespoon **balsamic vinegar**
2½ cups **baby arugula leaves**
salt and **black pepper**

Blanch the broccoli in a saucepan of lightly salted boiling water for 2 minutes. Drain well and refresh under cold water. Drain again, pat dry, and set aside.

Rub the beef with 1 tablespoon of the oil and season well with salt and pepper.

Heat a ridged griddle pan until very hot, add the beef, and cook over a high heat for 2 minutes on each side. Remove and allow to rest for 5 minutes, then cut into thick slices.

While the beef is resting, reheat the griddle pan, add the sourdough bread slices and cook for 2 minutes on each side until lightly charred.

Heat the remaining oil in a wok or large skillet, add the garlic and chili, and stir-fry for 1 minute. Add the broccoli and stir-fry for 1 minute. Stir in the vinegar and remove from heat. Combine with the beef and arugula in a large bowl.

Arrange the bread on serving plates, top with the beef salad, and serve.

For beef bruschetta with horseradish dressing, prepare and cook the beef as above. While the beef is resting, lightly chargrill the sourdough bread as above. Combine the sliced beef with 2½ cups picked watercress leaves in a large bowl. Arrange the bread on serving plates and top with the beef and watercress. Beat together 2 tablespoons sour cream, 2 teaspoons horseradish sauce, 1 teaspoon white wine vinegar, and salt and pepper to taste. Drizzle over the bruschetta and serve.

soy & orange salmon with noodles

Serves **4**
Preparation time **5 minutes**
Cooking time **15 minutes**

4 **skinless salmon fillets**,
    about 6 oz each
spray olive oil, for oiling
8 oz **dried soba noodles**
4 tablespoons **dark soy
    sauce**
2 tablespoons **orange juice**
2 tablespoons **mirin** (rice
    wine seasoning)
2 teaspoons **sesame oil**
2 tablespoons **sesame
    seeds**

Remove any bones from the salmon fillets and put the salmon in a bowl.

Heat a heavy skillet until hot and spray lightly with spray oil. Add the salmon and cook for 3–4 minutes on each side until browned. Remove, wrap loosely in foil, and let rest for 5 minutes.

Meanwhile, plunge the noodles into a large saucepan of boiling water. Return to a boil and cook for about 5 minutes, or until just tender. Drain well and toss with the sesame oil and seeds.

While the noodles are cooking, combine the soy sauce, orange juice, and mirin. Pour into the skillet and bring to a boil, then reduce the heat and simmer for 1 minute.

Divide the noodles between serving bowls and top each with the salmon and sauce. Serve with steamed sugar snap peas.

For salmon, orange, & soy parcels, put each salmon fillet on a 12 inch square of foil. Draw the foil edges up to form "cups" and add the soy sauce, orange juice, and mirin as above, along with 2 sliced scallions, 2 sliced garlic cloves, and 2 teaspoons grated fresh ginger root. Seal the edges of the foil together to form parcels, transfer to a baking sheet and bake in a preheated oven, 400°F, for 15 minutes. Remove and allow to rest briefly, then serve with steamed rice.

lamb with olive & pine nut salsa

Serves **4**
Preparation time **10 minutes**
Cooking time **9 minutes**

4 **lamb loin chops**, about
   7 oz each
1 tablespoon **extra virgin
   olive oil**
4 teaspoons **dried oregano**

Olive & pine nut salsa
3 tablespoons **extra virgin
   olive oil**
2 tablespoons **pine nuts**,
   toasted
⅔ cup **pitted black olives**,
   halved
2 tablespoons drained
   capers in brine
2 tablespoons chopped
   parsley
1 tablespoon **lemon juice**
salt and **black pepper**
arugula leaves, to garnish

Make the salsa. Heat 1 tablespoon of the oil in a
small skillet, add the pine nuts, and cook gently
for 30 seconds until golden. Allow to cool.

Combine the cooled pine nuts with the olives, capers,
parsley, lemon juice, and remaining oil in a bowl and
season to taste with salt and pepper.

Brush the chops with the oil and season with the
oregano and salt and pepper. Heat a ridged griddle
pan until hot, add the chops, and cook for 4 minutes
on each side.

Remove the chops from the pan, wrap loosely in foil,
and let rest for 5 minutes. Serve with the salsa.

For lamb chops with tomato, mint, & feta salad,
follow the recipe above to cook the chops. Meanwhile,
combine 4 diced tomatoes, 1 crushed garlic clove,
4 oz crumbled feta cheese, ⅓ cup pitted black olives,
2 tablespoons chopped mint leaves, 2 tablespoons
extra virgin olive oil, 2 teaspoons balsamic vinegar,
and salt and pepper to taste in a bowl. Stir well and
serve with the lamb.

chicken & hummus wraps

Serves **4**
Preparation time **5 minutes**
Cooking time **10 minutes**

6 **skinless chicken thigh
  fillets**, about 1 lb in total
2 tablespoons **extra virgin
  olive oil**
grated **zest** and **juice** of
  1 lemon
1 **garlic clove**, crushed
1 teaspoon **ground cumin**
4 **flour tortillas**
¾ cup store-bought **hummus**
  (see below for homemade)
½ cup **wild arugula leaves**
1 handful **parsley leaves**
salt and **black pepper**

Cut the chicken thighs into quarters and put in a bowl. Combine the oil, lemon zest, garlic, cumin, and salt and pepper to taste, add to the chicken, and stir well.

Heat a ridged griddle pan until hot. Thread the chicken pieces onto metal skewers, add to the pan, and cook for 4–5 minutes on each side. Remove and allow to rest for 5 minutes.

Meanwhile, warm the tortillas in a preheated oven, 350°F, for 5 minutes.

Remove the chicken from the skewers. Divide the hummus, arugula leaves, parsley, and chicken between the tortillas. Squeeze over the lemon juice, wrap, and serve.

For easy homemade hummus, put 13 oz can chickpeas, drained, 1 crushed garlic clove, 3 tablespoons extra virgin olive oil, 1 tablespoon lemon juice, and salt and pepper to taste in a food processor or blender and process until smooth.

hoisin pork stir-fry

Serves **2**
Preparation time **8 minutes**
Cooking time **6–8 minutes**

1 tablespoon **hoisin sauce**
1 tablespoon **light soy sauce**
1 tablespoon **white wine
vinegar**
1 tablespoon **vegetable oil**
2 **garlic cloves**, sliced
1 teaspoon grated **fresh
ginger root**
1 small **red chili**, seeded and
sliced
8 oz **pork tenderloin**, thinly
sliced
6 oz **sugar snap peas**
¾ cup **broccoli florets**
2 tablespoons **water**

Combine the hoisin and soy sauces and vinegar in a bowl and set aside.

Heat the oil in a wok or large skillet until starting to smoke, add the garlic, ginger, and chili and stir-fry over a high heat for 10 seconds. Add the pork tenderloin and stir-fry for 2–3 minutes until golden. Remove with a slotted spoon.

Add the sugar snap peas and broccoli florets to the pan and stir-fry for 1 minute. Add the measurement water and cook for 1 minute more.

Return the pork to the pan, add the sauce mixture, and cook for 1 minute until the vegetables are cooked. Serve with steamed rice.

For roasted hoisin pork, make the hoisin mixture as above. Brush the sauce over 4 pieces of pork tenderloin, about 6 oz each, in a roasting pan and roast in a preheated oven, 400°F, for 15 minutes. Allow to rest for 5 minutes, then serve with steamed green vegetables and boiled rice.

tuna & pesto burgers

Serves **4**
Preparation time **5 minutes**
Cooking time **4–6 minutes**

4 **ciabatta rolls**
4 **fresh tuna steaks**, about
　6 oz each
1 tablespoon **extra virgin**
　olive oil, plus extra to
　drizzle
1 **lemon**, halved
2 **tomatoes**, sliced
4 tablespoons **basil pesto**
1 cup **mixed salad leaves**
salt and **black pepper**

Heat a ridged griddle pan until hot. Split the rolls in half, add to pan, and cook for 1–2 minutes on each side until lightly charred. Transfer to serving plates.

Brush the tuna steaks lightly with the oil and season with salt and pepper. Add to the pan and cook for 1 minute on each side.

Transfer each tuna steak to the base of a roll and squeeze over a little lemon juice from the lemon halves. Divide the tomato slices, pesto, and salad leaves between the roll bases and drizzle over a little extra oil. Replace the roll tops and serve immediately.

For chicken & sweet chili burgers, split and lightly char the rolls on a hot ridged griddle pan as above. Cut 2 large skinless chicken breast fillets in half horizontally to give 4 thinner fillets. Brush the chicken with 1 tablespoon extra virgin olive oil and season with salt and pepper. Add to the hot pan and cook for 3 minutes on each side. Transfer a piece of chicken to each roll half and add 1 tablespoon sweet chili sauce and a small handful of mixed salad leaves.

mussels with cider

Serves **2**
Preparation time **10 minutes**
Cooking time **9 minutes**

3 lb small **farmed mussels**
2 **garlic cloves**, chopped
⅔ cup **hard cider**
6 tablespoons **heavy cream**
2 tablespoons chopped
 parsley
salt and **black pepper**

Wash the mussels thoroughly and put in a large saucepan with the garlic and cider. Bring to a boil, cover, and cook over a medium heat for 4–5 minutes until all the shells have opened. Discard any that remain closed after cooking.

Strain the mussels through a colander and put in a large bowl, cover with foil, and place in a very low oven to keep warm.

Pass the cooking juices through a fine sieve into a clean saucepan and bring to a boil. Beat in the cream and simmer for 3–4 minutes, or until thickened slightly. Season to taste with salt and pepper.

Pour the sauce over the mussels, sprinkle with the parsley, and serve immediately with plenty of crusty French bread to mop up the juices.

For mussels with Asian flavors, wash the mussels thoroughly and put in a large saucepan with 2 sliced garlic cloves, 2 teaspoons grated fresh ginger root, 4 sliced scallions, and 1 sliced red chili. Add a splash of water and cook as above. Strain the mussels and keep warm. Strain the cooking juices through a fine sieve into a clean saucepan. Beat in 6 tablespoons coconut cream and heat through. Pour over the mussels and serve garnished with chopped fresh cilantro.

mustard & tarragon pork steaks

Serves **4**
Preparation time **5 minutes**
Cooking time **10–12 minutes**

8 **pork steaks**, about 4 oz
   each
1 tablespoon **butter**
1 tablespoon **extra virgin
   olive oil**
⅔ cup **chicken stock**
½ cup **heavy cream**
4 teaspoons **wholegrain
   mustard**
1 tablespoon **chopped fresh
   tarragon**
salt and **black pepper**

Season the steaks on both sides with salt and pepper.

Heat the butter and oil together in a large skillet and as soon as the butter stops foaming add the steaks. Cook over a medium heat for 3–4 minutes each side until golden. Remove from the pan and wrap loosely in foil. Rest for 5 minutes.

Add the stock to the pan and simmer for 3 minutes then stir in the cream and mustard and simmer gently for 1–2 minutes until thickened slightly. Add the tarragon and remove from the heat.

Arrange the pork on plates, pour over the sauce, and serve with some steamed green vegetables, if desired.

For mustard & honey chicken, combine 1 tablespoon wholegrain mustard, 1 tablespoon honey, and some salt and pepper. Brush over 4 skinless chicken breast fillets and bake in a preheated oven, 400°F, for 15 minutes. Serve with green beans.

chili thai beef baguettes

Serves **4**
Preparation time **5 minutes**
Cooking time **4 minutes**

1 lb **thick sirloin steak**,
  trimmed
1 tablespoon **olive oil**
4 **oval bread rolls**
4 **cilantro sprigs**
4 **Thai** or **ordinary basil
  sprigs**
4 **mint sprigs**

Dressing
2 tablespoons **Thai fish
  sauce**
2 tablespoons **lime juice**
2 tablespoons **light brown
  sugar**
1 large **red chili**, thinly sliced
salt and **black pepper**

Heat a ridged griddle pan until very hot. Brush the steak with the oil and season liberally with salt and pepper. Add the steak to the pan and cook over a high heat for 2 minutes on each side, making sure that you sear all over. Allow to rest for 5 minutes, then cut into thin slices. The steak should be rare.

Meanwhile, make the dressing. Place the fish sauce, lime juice, and sugar in a bowl and stir in the chili until the sugar has dissolved.

Split the rolls in half and fill with the herbs, beef slices, and any juices. Pour the dressing carefully over and serve.

For Thai beef salad, cook, rest, and slice the steak as above. Toss with 1 sliced Lebanese cucumber, 8 oz halved cherry tomatoes, 1 ½ cups bean sprouts and 1 handful each of Thai or ordinary basil, cilantro, and mint leaves in a bowl. Combine the juice of ½ lime, 1 teaspoon sesame oil, 1 teaspoon superfine sugar, 1 teaspoon Thai fish sauce, and 1 tablespoon peanut oil. Add to the salad, toss well until evenly coated, and serve.

tortilla pizza with salami

Makes **2**
Preparation time **5 minutes**
Cooking time **8–10 minutes**
  per pizza

2 large **flour tortillas** or
  flatbreads
4 tablespoons store-bought
  tomato pasta sauce
4 oz **spicy salami slices**
5 oz **mozzarella cheese**,
  thinly sliced
1 tablespoon **oregano
  leaves**, plus extra to
  garnish
salt and **black pepper**

Lay the tortillas or flatbreads on 2 large baking sheets. Top each with half the pasta sauce, spreading it up to the edge. Arrange half the salami and mozzarella slices and oregano leaves over the top.

Bake in a preheated oven, 400°F, for 8–10 minutes until the cheese is melted and golden. Serve garnished with extra oregano leaves.

For spicy salami, mozzarella, & tomato quesadilla, lay 1 large flour tortilla or flatbread on the work surface. Top with 2 tablespoons tomato pasta sauce, 2 oz salami slices, 3 oz diced mozzarella cheese, and a few basil leaves. Add a second tortilla and press flat. Heat a large skillet or ridged griddle pan until hot, add the quesadilla, and cook for 2–3 minutes until toasted. Flip over and cook on the second side. Cut into wedges to serve.

chili & lemon shrimp with pasta

Serves **2**
Preparation time **5 minutes**,
  plus marinating
Cooking time **3 minutes**

3 tablespoons **extra virgin
  olive oil**, plus extra for
  stir-frying
2 large **garlic cloves**,
  crushed
1 large **red chili**, seeded and
  chopped
grated **zest** and **juice** of
  1 **lemon**
12 oz large **raw peeled
  shrimp**
8 oz **fresh spaghetti**
4 **scallions**, sliced
2 tablespoons chopped
  basil
salt and **black pepper**

Combine the oil, garlic, chili, lemon zest, and salt and pepper to taste in a nonmetallic bowl, add the shrimp, and stir well. Cover and allow to marinate in the refrigerator for 1 hour.

Cook the pasta in a large saucepan of salted boiling water for about 3 minutes until al dente, then drain.

Meanwhile, heat a wok or large skillet until hot and add a drizzle of oil. Tip in the shrimp mixture and the scallions and stir-fry over a high heat for 2–3 minutes until the shrimp are lightly browned. Add the lemon juice and basil and stir well.

Serve the shrimp immediately with the cooked pasta.

For spicy Asian shrimp with jasmine rice, combine the oil, garlic, and chili as above with the grated zest of 1 lime and 2 teaspoons grated fresh ginger root. Add the shrimp and stir well. Let marinate as above. Put ¾ cup jasmine rice in a small saucepan, cover with 1¼ cups cold water, and add a little salt. Bring to a boil, then reduce the heat, cover with a tight-fitting lid, and simmer over a very low heat for 12 minutes. Remove from the heat and allow to stand for 10 minutes. Meanwhile, stir-fry the shrimp and scallions as above, but add 1 tablespoon light soy sauce just before the shrimp are cooked. Add the juice of the lime and 2 tablespoons chopped fresh cilantro and stir well. Fluff up the rice and serve with the shrimp mixture.

pasta, rice, & noodles

creamy tuna & leek pasta

Serves **4**
Preparation time **10 minutes**
Cooking time **12 minutes**

13 oz **dried penne**
2 tablespoons **extra virgin olive oil**
2 **leeks**, sliced
2 large **garlic cloves**, sliced
2 x 7 oz cans **tuna in olive oil**, drained
⅔ cup **dry white wine**
⅔ cup **heavy cream**
2 tablespoons chopped **parsley**
salt and **black pepper**

Plunge the pasta into a large saucepan of lightly salted boiling water. Return to a boil and cook for 10–12 minutes until al dente. Drain well and return to the pan.

Meanwhile, heat the oil in a skillet, add the leeks, garlic, and salt and pepper to taste and cook gently for 5 minutes.

Flake in the tuna and cook, stirring, for 1 minute. Add the wine, bring to a boil, and boil until reduced by half. Stir in the cream and heat through for 2–3 minutes.

Add the tuna sauce to the pasta with the parsley and stir over a medium heat for 1 minute. Serve immediately with an arugula salad.

For chicken, leek, & arugula pasta, while the pasta is cooking as above, heat 4 tablespoons extra virgin olive oil in a skillet, add 2 sliced leeks, 2 crushed garlic cloves, and 2 seeded and sliced red chilies and cook gently for 5 minutes. Add 8 oz diced skinless chicken breast fillets and cook over a medium-high heat for about 5 minutes, or until golden and cooked through. Stir into the cooked, drained pasta with 3 cups arugula leaves, a squeeze of lemon juice, and a little extra oil. Serve immediately.

sausage meatballs, peas, & pasta

Serves **4**
Preparation time **20 minutes**
Cooking time **15 minutes**

1 lb **beef** or **pork sausages**,
skins removed
4 tablespoons **extra virgin
olive oil**
2 **garlic cloves**, sliced
2 tablespoons chopped
sage
½ teaspoon **dried red pepper
flakes**
13 oz **dried fusilli**
1⅔ cups **frozen peas**,
thawed
salt and **black pepper**
freshly grated **Parmesan
cheese**, to serve

Cut the sausagemeat into small pieces and roll into walnut-size meatballs.

Heat half the oil in a large nonstick skillet, add the meatballs, and cook over a medium heat, stirring frequently, for 10 minutes until cooked through. Remove from the pan with a slotted spoon.

Meanwhile, plunge the pasta into a large saucepan of lightly salted boiling water. Return to a boil and cook for 8 minutes. Add the peas, return to a boil, and cook for 2 minutes more until the peas are just tender and the pasta is al dente. Drain well, reserving 4 tablespoons of the cooking water.

Add the garlic, sage, pepper flakes, and salt and pepper to taste to the meatball pan and cook over a low heat for 2–3 minutes until the garlic is soft but not browned. Return the meatballs to the pan.

Return the pasta and peas to the pan and stir in the meatball mixture, reserved cooking water, and remaining oil and heat through for 2 minutes. Serve in bowls topped with grated Parmesan.

For shrimp, chorizo, peas, & pasta, cook the pasta and peas as above. Meanwhile heat a dry skillet until hot, add 5 oz diced chorizo, and fry over high heat for 3–4 minutes until the fat is released. Lower the heat, add 12 oz peeled raw shrimp and 2 crushed garlic cloves, and stir-fry over a low heat for 5 minutes until the shrimp are cooked. Stir this into the drained pasta and peas along with 4 tablespoons chopped fresh mint, juice of ½ lemon, and a drizzle of extra virgin olive oil. Season to taste and serve.

macaroni cheese with chorizo

Serves **4**
Preparation time **5 minutes**
Cooking time **30 minutes**

8 oz **dried macaroni**
4 oz **chorizo**, diced
1 small **onion**, finely
   chopped
1 **garlic clove**, crushed
1¼ cups **heavy cream**
⅔ cup **chicken stock** (see
   page 44 for homemade)
¾ cup grated **cheddar**
   cheese
4 tablespoons freshly grated
   Parmesan cheese
salt and **black pepper**

Plunge the pasta into a saucepan of lightly salted boiling water. Return to a boil and simmer for 10–12 minutes until al dente. Drain well and return to the pan.

Meanwhile, heat a dry skillet until hot, add the chorizo, and cook for 3 minutes until browned and the fat is released. Remove from the pan with a slotted spoon. Add the onion and garlic to the pan and cook gently for 5 minutes until soft.

Stir in the macaroni with the chorizo, cream, stock, and a little salt and pepper. Heat gently, stirring, for 2–3 minutes until warmed through. Stir in the cheddar, remove the pan from the heat, and stir until the cheese has melted.

Spoon the mixture into 4 x 1¼ cup baking dishes, sprinkle with the Parmesan, and bake in a preheated oven, 375°F, for 12–15 minutes until bubbling and golden. Serve with a crisp green salad.

For cheesy baked pasta with bacon, cook 8 oz dried penne until al dente instead of the macaroni, and cook 4 oz diced bacon in place of the chorizo as above. Cook the onion and garlic as above, then stir in the penne, cream, and salt and pepper and heat through for 2–3 minutes. Stir in ¾ cup grated Gruyère cheese, remove from the heat, and stir until melted. Spoon the pasta mixture into a 4 cup baking dish, sprinkle with the Parmesan, and bake in a preheated oven, 375°F, for 25 minutes.

singapore chicken noodles

Serves **4**
Preparation time **10 minutes**,
  plus marinating
Cooking time **5–6 minutes**

12 oz **skinless chicken thigh
  fillets**, sliced
2 tablespoons **light soy
  sauce**
1 tablespoon **superfine
  sugar**
1 teaspoon **sesame oil**
2 tablespoons **oyster sauce**
2 tablespoons **rice wine
  vinegar**
3 tablespoons **vegetable oil**
4 **scallions**, thickly sliced
2 **garlic cloves**, sliced
1 teaspoon grated **fresh
  ginger root**
12 oz **fresh hokkein noodles**
1 cup **bean sprouts**
sliced **red chilies**, to garnish

Put the chicken in a bowl. Add the soy sauce, sugar, and sesame oil and stir well. Cover and allow to marinate at cool room temperature for 15 minutes.

Strain the chicken and reserve the marinade. Add the oyster sauce and rice wine vinegar to the marinade and set aside.

Heat half the vegetable oil in a wok or large skillet until starting to smoke. Add the chicken and stir-fry over a high heat for 2–3 minutes until lightly golden. Remove from the pan with a slotted spoon.

Heat the remaining oil in the pan, add the scallions, garlic, and ginger and stir-fry over a high heat for 1 minute. Return the chicken to the pan with the noodles and marinade mixture and toss for 2 minutes until heated through.

Stir through the bean sprouts and serve in bowls, garnished with red chili slices.

For barbecued Asian chicken, put the chicken slices in a bowl and add 2 tablespoons light soy sauce, ½ teaspoon sesame oil, 1 tablespoon oyster sauce, and 1 teaspoon honey. Stir well until the chicken is evenly coated. Thread onto metal skewers and cook under a preheated high broiler or on a preheated hot barbecue for 4–5 minutes on each side. Serve with a salad.

pad thai

Serves **2**
Preparation time **10 minutes**
Cooking time **12 minutes**

8 oz **dried rice noodles**
1½ tablespoons **sweet soy sauce**
1½ tablespoons **lime juice**
1 tablespoon **Thai fish sauce**
1 tablespoon **water**
3 tablespoons **peanut oil**
2 **garlic cloves**, sliced
1 small **red chili**, seeded and chopped
4 oz **firm tofu**, diced
2 **eggs**, lightly beaten
2 cups **bean sprouts**
1 tablespoon chopped **cilantro**
4 tablespoons **salted peanuts**, chopped

Cook the noodles in boiling water for 5 minutes until softened. Drain and immediately refresh under cold water, drain again, and set aside.

Combine the soy sauce, lime juice, fish sauce, and measurement water in a small bowl and set aside.

Heat the oil in a wok or large skillet, add the garlic and chili, and stir-fry over a medium heat for 30 seconds. Add the noodles and tofu and stir-fry for 2–3 minutes until heated through.

Carefully push the noodle mixture up the side of the pan, clearing the center of the pan. Add the eggs and heat gently for 1 minute without stirring, then gently start "scrambling" the eggs with a spoon. Mix the noodles back into the center and stir well until mixed with the eggs.

Add the soy sauce mixture and cook for 1 minute, or until heated through. Stir in the bean sprouts and cilantro. Spoon into bowls and serve immediately, topped with the peanuts.

For fresh noodle salad, cook 8 oz dried rice noodles as above. Put in a bowl and add 1 shredded carrot, ½ sliced cucumber, 1 handful of bean sprouts, and 1 handful each of basil, mint, and fresh cilantro leaves. Combine 1 teaspoon sesame oil, 2 tablespoons olive oil, 1 tablespoon Thai fish sauce, 2 teaspoons superfine sugar, and 1 tablespoon lime juice. Stir into the salad and serve garnished with 4 tablespoons chopped toasted peanuts.

sweet & sour pork noodles

Serves **2**
Preparation time **10 minutes**,
  plus marinating
Cooking time **6–7 minutes**

8 oz **pork tenderloin**
3 tablespoons **light soy sauce**
2 tablespoons **sweet chili sauce**
1 tablespoon **superfine sugar**
1 tablespoon **rice wine vinegar**
3 tablespoons **vegetable oil**
2 **garlic cloves**, sliced
2 teaspoons grated **fresh ginger root**
1 small **onion**, sliced
1 **red bell pepper**, cored, seeded, and sliced
8 oz **fresh hokkein noodles**

Cut the pork into thin slices and put in a bowl. Combine the soy and chili sauces, sugar, and vinegar and add to the pork. Stir well until the pork is evenly coated, cover, and allow to marinate at cool room temperature for 15 minutes. Strain the pork, reserve the marinade, and set aside.

Heat half the oil in a wok or large skillet until starting to smoke. Add the pork and stir-fry over a high heat for 3–4 minutes until golden. Remove from the pan with a slotted spoon.

Heat the remaining oil in the pan, add the garlic, ginger, onion, and red pepper and stir-fry over a high heat for 1 minute. Return the pork to the pan with the noodles and marinade and toss for 2 minutes until heated through. Serve immediately.

For chicken with plum sauce & noodles, thinly slice 8 oz skinless chicken breast fillets and put in a bowl. Combine 1 tablespoon light soy sauce, 2 tablespoons plum sauce, and the juice of ½ lime and add to the chicken. Stir well until the chicken is evenly coated, cover, and let marinate at cool room temperature for 15 minutes. Use as for the pork above, but replace the bell pepper with ½ cup broccoli florets. Serve the chicken and noodles garnished with fresh cilantro leaves.

everything rice

Serves **6**
Preparation time **20 minutes**
Cooking time **45–50 minutes**

2 lb **chicken**, jointed into 12
    pieces (ask your butcher)
1 tablespoon **jerk seasoning**
4 tablespoons **olive oil**
1 **onion**, chopped
1 **red bell pepper**, cored,
    seeded, and chopped
2 **celery sticks**, chopped
2 **garlic cloves**, crushed
1 tablespoon chopped
    thyme
1¼ cups **long-grain rice**
2½ cups hot **chicken stock**
    (see page 44 for
    homemade)
8 oz **piece of cooked ham**,
    diced
8 oz **raw peeled shrimp**
2 tablespoons chopped
    cilantro

Put the chicken pieces in a bowl, add the jerk
seasoning and salt and pepper, and stir well to
evenly coat the chicken.

Heat the oil in a skillet, add the chicken pieces, and
cook for 5–6 minutes until browned all over. Remove
from the pan with a slotted spoon.

Add the onion, red pepper, celery, garlic, thyme, and
salt and pepper to taste to the pan and cook, stirring
frequently, for 10 minutes until golden. Return the
chicken to the pan.

Add the rice and stir well, then add the hot stock. Bring
to a boil, then reduce the heat, cover, and simmer
gently for 20 minutes.

Stir in the ham and shrimp and cook, covered, for an
additional 10 minutes until the rice is tender and all the
stock has been absorbed. Adjust the seasoning and
serve immediately.

For classic paella, prepare and cook the chicken and
vegetables as above. After returning the chicken to the
pan, add 1¼ cups paella rice and stir well. Add the hot
stock with 13 oz can chopped tomatoes. Bring to a
boil, then reduce the heat, cover, and simmer gently
for 35–40 minutes until the rice is creamy and tender
and most of the stock has been absorbed. Adjust the
seasoning and serve immediately.

pea & shrimp risotto

Serves **6**
Preparation time **10 minutes**
Cooking time **40 minutes**

1 lb **raw shrimp in their
  shells**
½ cup **butter**
1 **onion**, finely chopped
2 **garlic cloves**, crushed
1¼ cups **risotto rice**
2½ cups **fresh peas**
⅔ cup **dry white wine**
6 cups hot **vegetable stock**
  (see page 58 for
  homemade)
4 tablespoons chopped **mint**
salt and **black pepper**

Peel the shrimp, reserving the heads and shells.

Melt all but 1 tablespoon butter in a large skillet and
fry the shrimp heads and shells for 3–4 minutes.
Strain and return butter to the pan, discarding heads
and shells.

Add the onion and garlic and cook for 5 minutes until
softened but not browned. Add the rice and stir well
to coat the grains with the butter. Add the peas, then
pour in the wine. Bring to a boil and cook, stirring, until
reduced by half.

Add the hot stock, a large ladleful at a time, and
cook, stirring constantly until each addition has been
absorbed before adding the next. Continue in this way
until all the stock has been absorbed and the rice is
creamy but the grains are still firm. This should take
about 20 minutes.

Melt the remaining butter in a separate skillet, add
the shrimp, and cook, stirring, for 3–4 minutes. Stir
into the rice with the pan juices and mint and season
to taste with salt and pepper.

For pea & shrimp risotto cakes, cook the risotto
as above, then allow to go cold. Stir in 2 beaten eggs
and ½ cup grated Parmesan cheese. Using damp
hands, shape the mixture into 4 inch patties. Heat
a shallow depth of vegetable oil in a skillet, add the
cakes, in batches, and cook for 3–4 minutes on each
side until golden brown and heated through. Remove
from the pan with a slotted spoon and keep warm in a
preheated oven, 300°F, while you cook the remainder.
Serve with a crisp green salad.

baked risotto with burnt butter

Serves **4–6**
Preparation time **5 minutes**
Cooking time **40 minutes**

spray olive oil, for oiling
1¾ cups **risotto rice**
5 cups hot **chicken stock**
  (see page 44 for
  homemade)
¼ cup **butter**
½ cup **Parmesan cheese**,
  freshly grated
salt and **black pepper**

Spray an 8 cup casserole lightly with spray oil. Put the rice in the prepared dish and pour over the stock. Add a little salt and pepper, stir once, and cover with a tight-fitting lid (add a layer of foil if necessary).

Bake in a preheated oven, 350°F, for 40 minutes until the rice is tender and most of the stock has been absorbed.

Meanwhile, melt the butter in a small saucepan and cook gently for 2–3 minutes until the butter browns to a nutty color.

Remove the risotto from the oven and stir in the Parmesan and the browned butter. Serve immediately.

For baked pumpkin risotto, combine 1 lb peeled, seeded, and diced pumpkin in a roasting pan with 1 thinly sliced onion, 1 crushed garlic clove, 1 tablespoon chopped sage, 2 tablespoons extra virgin olive oil, and salt and pepper to taste. Prepare the rice ready for baking as above and put in the oven, with the pumpkin mixture on the shelf below the risotto. After baking for 40 minutes, stir the pumpkin mixture and ½ cup freshly grated Parmesan cheese into the baked risotto, then the browned butter as above.

meat, poultry, & fish

herb & bacon chicken roast

Serves **4**
Preparation time **10 minutes**
Cooking time **45 minutes**

2 tablespoons **extra virgin
olive oil**
2 tablespoons chopped
thyme
2 **garlic cloves**, crushed
grated **zest** and **juice** of
1 **lemon**
4 **chicken quarters**, about
12 oz each
4 **bacon slices**, rind removed
1 tablespoon **all-purpose
flour**
⅔ cup **dry white wine**
1¼ pints **chicken stock** (see
page 44 for homemade)
salt and **black pepper**

Combine the oil, thyme, garlic, lemon zest, and salt and pepper to taste in a bowl. Score the chicken quarters several times with a sharp knife and rub all over with the oil and herb mixture. Wrap each chicken quarter with bacon using toothpicks to secure in place.

Transfer to a roasting pan and roast in a preheated oven, 400°F, for 35–40 minutes until crisp and golden. Remove from the oven, transfer the chicken pieces to a warm platter, and wrap with foil.

Pour off all but 2 tablespoons fat from the roasting pan and place the pan over a medium heat. Add the flour and cook, stirring constantly, for 30 seconds. Gradually stir in the wine and then the stock and simmer for 5 minutes until thickened. Serve with the chicken.

For perfect roast potatoes to serve with the chicken, cook 1½ lb peeled potatoes in a large saucepan of lightly salted boiling water for 10 minutes. Drain well, return to the pan, and shake firmly to fluff up the edges. Put 4 tablespoons olive oil in a roasting pan and heat in a preheated oven, 400°F, for 5 minutes. Carefully tip in the potatoes (the oil will spit) and roast in the oven for 45–50 minutes, stirring halfway through, until crisp and golden.

chicken with red wine & grapes

Serves **4**
Preparation time **5 minutes**
Cooking time **30 minutes**

3 tablespoons **olive oil**
4 **skinless chicken breast fillets**, about 5 oz each
1 **red onion**, sliced
2 tablespoons **red pesto** (see below for homemade)
1¼ cups **red wine**
1¼ cups **water**
¾ cup **red grapes**, halved and seeded
salt and **black pepper**
basil leaves, to garnish

Heat 2 tablespoons of the oil in a large skillet, add the chicken breasts and cook over a medium heat for 5 minutes, turning frequently, until browned all over. Remove from the pan with a slotted spoon and drain on paper towels.

Heat the remaining oil in the pan, add the onion slices and pesto, and cook, stirring constantly, for 3 minutes until the onion is softened but not browned.

Add the wine and measurement water to the pan and bring to a boil. Return the chicken breasts to the pan and season with salt and pepper to taste. Reduce the heat and simmer for 15 minutes, or until the chicken is cooked through.

Stir in the grapes and serve immediately, garnished with basil leaves.

For homemade red pesto, put 1 chopped garlic clove, ½ teaspoon sea salt, ¾ cup basil leaves, 1 cup drained sundried tomatoes in oil, ½ cup extra virgin olive oil, and a little pepper in a food processor or blender and blend until smooth. Transfer to a bowl and stir in 2 tablespoons freshly grated Parmesan cheese.

chicken thighs with fresh pesto

Serves **4**
Preparation time **10 minutes**
Cooking time **25 minutes**

1 tablespoon **olive oil**
8 **chicken thighs**

Green pesto
6 tablespoons **olive oil**
⅓ cup **pine nuts**, toasted
½ cup freshly grated
   Parmesan cheese
1 ¼ **basil leaves**, plus extra to
   garnish
¼ cup **flat-leaf parsley**
2 **garlic cloves**, chopped
salt and **black pepper**

Heat the oil in a nonstick skillet, add the chicken thighs, and cook over a medium heat, turning frequently, for about 20 minutes or until the chicken is cooked through.

Meanwhile, make the pesto. Put all the ingredients in a food processor or blender and process until smooth.

Remove the chicken from the pan and keep hot. Reduce the heat and add the pesto to the pan. Heat through, stirring, for 2–3 minutes.

Pour the warmed pesto over the chicken thighs, garnish with basil, and serve with steamed vegetables and roasted cherry tomatoes.

For chicken thighs with mustard & sour cream sauce, cook the chicken thighs as above, remove from the skillet, and keep warm. Reduce the heat, add 3 tablespoons dry white wine, and scrape the base of the pan to loosen the residue. Simmer until reduced by half. Stir in ½ cup sour cream and 1 tablespoon wholegrain mustard and heat through, stirring, for 3 minutes. Pour over the chicken and serve garnished with chopped fresh chives.

chicken satay

Serves **6**
Preparation time **10 minutes**,
  plus marinating
Cooking time **10 minutes**

2 tablespoons **smooth
  peanut butter**
½ cup **soy sauce**
½ cup **lime juice**
2–3 tablespoons **curry
  powder**
2 **garlic cloves**, chopped
1 teaspoon **hot pepper
  sauce**
6 **skinless chicken breast
  fillets**, cubed

Combine the peanut butter, soy sauce, lime juice, curry powder, garlic, and hot pepper sauce in a large nonmetallic bowl.

Add the chicken to the marinade and stir well until evenly coated. Cover and allow to marinate in the refrigerator for about 12 hours or overnight.

When ready to cook, thread the chicken onto metal skewers and cook under a preheated high broiler for 5 minutes on each side, or until cooked through. Serve immediately.

For piri piri chicken skewers, combine 4 tablespoons extra virgin olive oil, 2 chopped red chilies (seeded if wished), 2 crushed garlic cloves, and salt and pepper to taste in a large bowl. Reserve half the mixture separately, then add the chicken to the remaining half in the bowl and stir well until evenly coated. Cover and allow to marinate in the refrigerator for about 12 hours or overnight. Thread the chicken onto bamboo skewers, presoaked in boiling water for 10 minutes, and cook under a preheated high broiler for 5 minutes on each side, or until cooked through. Serve drizzled with the remaining piri piri and a squeeze of lemon juice.

duck breasts with lentils

Serves **4**
Preparation time **10 minutes**
Cooking time **25–30 minutes**

4 x **duck breasts**, about 6 oz
   each
¾ cup **Puy lentils**
⅔ cup **chicken stock** (see
   page 44 for homemade)
salt and **black pepper**
chervil sprigs, to garnish

Marmalade
1¼ cups **orange juice**
8 oz **mandarin oranges**,
   seeds removed but with
   peel left on, finely chopped

Sauce
3 **shallots**, finely chopped
3 tablespoons **port**
⅔ cup **red grape juice**

Put the duck breasts in a shallow roasting pan, skin side up, and roast in a preheated oven, 400°F, for 10–15 minutes—they should still be pink in the center. Allow to rest for 5 minutes.

Meanwhile, put the lentils in a saucepan of salted water, bring to a boil, and boil for 15 minutes, then drain.

While the duck and lentils are cooking, make the marmalade. Put the orange juice and mandarins in a stainless-steel saucepan. Bring to a boil, then reduce the heat and cook for 10 minutes, or until reduced by two-thirds. At the same time, for the sauce, heat a dry nonstick skillet, add the shallots, and cook gently for 2–3 minutes. Add the port and grape juice. Bring to a boil and boil for 10 minutes, or until reduced by half.

Remove the duck from the pan and set aside. Skim off the excess fat from the pan. Add the cooked lentils and stock and cook over a medium heat, scraping any residue from the pan, for 2–3 minutes until the stock has nearly all evaporated.

Slice the duck breasts. Divide the lentils between warmed plates and top with the duck slices. Spoon a little marmalade over the meat, pour the sauce around the lentils, and serve garnished with chervil sprigs.

lamb rogan josh

Serves **4**

Preparation time **20 minutes**, plus marinating

Cooking time **2 hours**

2 lb **boneless leg of lamb**

13 oz can **chopped tomatoes**

1¼ cups **water**

1 teaspoon **superfine sugar**

2 tablespoons chopped **cilantro**, plus extra to garnish

Marinade

1 **onion**, roughly chopped

4 **garlic cloves**, roughly chopped

2 teaspoons grated **fresh ginger root**

1 large **red chili**, chopped

2 teaspoons **ground coriander**

1½ teaspoons **salt**

1 teaspoon **ground cumin**

1 teaspoon **ground turmeric**

½ teaspoon **ground cinnamon**

½ teaspoon **ground white pepper**

2 tablespoons **red wine vinegar**

Cut the lamb into chunks, discarding any gristle, and put in a large nonmetallic bowl.

Make the marinade. Put all the ingredients in a food processor or blender and process to a smooth paste. Add to the lamb and stir well until evenly coated. Cover and allow to marinate in the refrigerator overnight.

When ready to cook, put the meat and all the marinade juices in a saucepan with the tomatoes, measurement water, and sugar. Bring to a boil, then reduce the heat, cover, and simmer gently for 1½ hours.

Stir in the cilantro and cook, uncovered, for an additional 25–30 minutes until the sauce is thickened. Adjust the seasoning, garnish with the cilantro, and serve with rice (see below).

For perfect rice to serve with the curry, put 1½ cups basmati rice in a large saucepan with 6 cups cold water and 1 teaspoon salt. Bring to a boil, then reduce the heat and simmer for 10 minutes. Drain the rice in a sieve and then place the sieve back over the pan. Cover the whole sieve and pan with a clean dish towel and let stand for 5 minutes. Fluff up the grains with a fork and serve.

lamb & zucchini koftas

Serves **4**
Preparation time **20 minutes**
Cooking time **20 minutes**

2 **zucchini**, finely grated
2 tablespoons **sesame seeds**
8 oz **ground lamb**
2 **scallions**, finely chopped
1 **garlic clove**, crushed
1 tablespoon chopped **mint**
½ teaspoon **ground mixed spice**
2 tablespoons **dried bread crumbs**
1 **egg**, lightly beaten
vegetable oil, for pan-frying
salt and **black pepper**
lemon wedges, to garnish

Put the zucchini in a sieve and press down to extract as much liquid as possible. Transfer to a bowl.

Heat a dry heavy skillet until hot, add the sesame seeds, and cook, shaking constantly, for 1–2 minutes until golden brown and aromatic. Add to the zucchini, together with the lamb and all the remaining ingredients, except the oil and lemon wedges. Season liberally with salt and pepper.

Form the mixture into 20 small balls. Heat a shallow depth of oil in a skillet, add the koftas, in batches, and cook for 5 minutes, turning frequently until evenly browned. Keep the cooked koftas warm in a preheated oven, 325°F, while you cook the remainder. Serve hot, garnished with lemon wedges.

For tahini sauce to serve as an accompaniment, combine 1 cup Greek or whole milk yogurt, 2 crushed garlic cloves, 1 tablespoon tahini paste, 2 teaspoons lemon juice, and salt and pepper to taste in a bowl.

mustard lamb loin

Serves **4**

Preparation time **10 minutes**,
plus resting

Cooking time **10–15 minutes**

1 lb **boneless loin of lamb**
4 **garlic cloves**, crushed
2 tablespoons **Dijon** or
English mustard
2 tablespoons chopped **mint**
1 tablespoon chopped
cilantro
1 tablespoon **olive oil**

Trim the lamb of any fat.

Combine the garlic, mustard, mint, cilantro, and oil in a
small bowl.

Rub the lamb with the garlic and mustard mixture.
Transfer to a baking dish.

Bake in a preheated oven, 400°F, for 10–15 minutes,
or until the lamb is cooked to your taste. Let rest for
10 minutes, then serve with a selection of steamed
vegetables.

For sweet potato mash to serve with the lamb, cook
1 lb peeled sweet potatoes with 12 oz peeled potatoes
in a large saucepan of lightly salted boiling water
until tender. Drain well and return to the pan. Mash in
¼ cup butter, 3 tablespoons milk, and salt and pepper
to taste.

pork spare ribs

Serve **4**
Preparation time **5 minutes**
Cooking time **1 hour**

2 **pork spare rib racks**
  (about 2 lb each)
½ cup **tomato ketchup**
2 tablespoons **clear honey**
1 tablespoon **dark soy sauce**
1 tablespoon **olive oil**
1 tablespoon **malt vinegar**
2 teaspoons **Dijon mustard**
salt and **black pepper**

Arrange the ribs on a wire rack in a large roasting pan. Combine the remaining ingredients in a bowl. Brush the ribs generously on both sides with the marinade.

Roast the ribs in a preheated oven, 400°F, for 30 minutes.

Baste the ribs again on both sides with the marinade, using a clean brush, and roast for an additional 30 minutes until golden and sticky.

Remove from the oven, brush over the remaining marinade, and allow to cool for 5 minutes before serving, divided into 4 portions.

For Chinese hoisin wings, combine all the marinade ingredients from the recipe above in a bowl, but adding 2 tablespoons hoisin sauce. Mix with 12 large chicken wings to coat evenly. Roast the wings in a preheated oven, 400°F, for 30–35 minutes until crisp and golden and cooked through.

marinated pork tenderloin

Serves **4**
Preparation time **10 minutes**,
 plus marinating
Cooking time **20 minutes**

2 **pork tenderloins**, about
 8 oz each
1 tablespoon **flax seeds**
⅔ cup **dry white wine**

Marinade
1 **cinnamon stick**
2 tablespoons **soy sauce**
2 **garlic cloves**, crushed
1 teaspoon grated **fresh
 ginger root**
1 tablespoon **honey**
1 teaspoon crushed
 coriander seeds
1 teaspoon **sesame oil**

Combine the marinade ingredients in a bowl. Put the pork tenderloins in a shallow dish and coat evenly with the marinade. Cover and marinate in the refrigerator for at least 2–3 hours, and preferably overnight.

When ready to cook, drain the pork, reserving the marinade. Lay the pork in the flax seeds on both sides so that it is evenly covered. Heat a baking sheet or roasting pan on the stove top, add the pork, and cook over a high heat until browned and sealed on both sides. Transfer to a preheated oven, 350°F, and roast for 15 minutes, or until golden brown.

Meanwhile, remove the cinnamon stick from the marinade and pour the liquid into a nonstick saucepan. Add the wine and bring to a boil, then reduce the heat and simmer until it has the consistency of a sticky glaze. Remove the pan from the heat.

Cut the roasted pork into ¼ inch slices. Serve on a bed of steamed vegetables, such as bok choy or spinach, and drizzle the glaze over the pork.

For pork tenderloin with Dukhah crust, omit marinating the pork. Heat a dry skillet until hot, then dry fry 3 tablespoons sesame seeds, 2 tablespoons coriander seeds, and ½ tablespoon cumin seeds for 2 minutes until browned. Allow to cool, then grind in a spice grinder. Stir in 3 tablespoons toasted and chopped blanched almonds, ½ teaspoon salt, and a little pepper. Transfer to a plate and coat the pork tenderloins on both sides in the mixture. Roast the pork on a baking sheet or in a roasting pan as above. Rest for 5 minutes, then serve with a green salad.

asparagus & prosciutto wraps

Serves **3**
Preparation time **10 minutes**
Cooking time **28 minutes**

18 thick **asparagus spears**,
   trimmed
8 oz **mozzarella cheese**
8 oz thinly sliced **prosciutto**
⅓ cup **butter**, plus extra for
   greasing
black pepper

Plunge the asparagus into a large saucepan of salted boiling water, then cook over a medium heat for 4–8 minutes, or until just tender.

Drain and plunge into cold water. When cooled, drain again and set aside.

Cut the mozzarella into 18 equal slices. Separate the prosciutto slices into 6 even piles and cut the butter into 12 even-size pieces.

Take 3 asparagus spears and put them on 1 bundle of prosciutto. Put 2 pieces of mozzarella in between the spears, along with a piece of butter. Wrap the prosciutto around the asparagus, using all the slices in the pile. Repeat until you have 6 bundles.

Lightly grease an ovenproof dish and arrange the asparagus bundles over the base. Put a slice of mozzarella and a piece of butter on each bundle. Season with pepper and bake at the top of a preheated oven, 400°F, for 20 minutes.

For asparagus with lemon & garlic butter sauce, cook the asparagus spears as above. Meanwhile, put ½ cup butter, 1 crushed garlic clove, finely grated zest of 1 lemon, and a little pepper in a saucepan and cook gently until the garlic is soft. Beat in 1 tablespoon lemon juice and serve drizzled over the asparagus.

pork with savoy cabbage

Serves **4**
Preparation time **15 minutes**
Cooking time **40 minutes**

1 tablespoon **sesame seeds**
2 **garlic cloves**, very finely
sliced
3 **scallions**, diagonally sliced
into ¾ inch pieces
½ teaspoon **cayenne pepper**
10 oz **pork loin**, cut into
thick strips
2 tablespoons **olive oil**
2 teaspoons **sesame oil**
2 tablespoons **soy sauce**
2 teaspoons **honey**
3 cups shredded **Savoy
cabbage**

Heat a dry heavy skillet until hot, add the sesame
seeds, and cook, shaking constantly, for 1–2 minutes
until golden brown and aromatic. Remove to a cool
plate and set aside.

Combine the garlic, scallions, and cayenne pepper in a
bowl. Add the pork and mix well.

Heat the oils in a skillet, add the pork, in 3 batches, and
stir-fry over a high heat for 5 minutes on each side, or
until golden and cooked through. Remove from the pan
with a slotted spoon.

Add the soy sauce, honey, and cabbage to the pan and
toss to mix. Cover and cook over a medium heat for
5–6 minutes.

Return the pork to the pan, add the sesame seeds, and
toss well. Serve immediately.

For orange & mustard seed rice to serve with the
pork, put 1¼ cups jasmine rice in a saucepan and add
2 cups cold water and 1 teaspoon salt. Bring to a
boil, then reduce the heat, cover with a tight-fitting
lid, and simmer over a very low heat for 12 minutes.
Meanwhile, melt 2 tablespoons butter in a small
saucepan, add 1 tablespoon mustard seeds and
grated zest of 1 orange, and cook gently, stirring,
for 2–3 minutes until the mustard seeds turn golden.
Remove the rice from the heat, pour in the mustard
seed mixture, and replace the lid. Allow to stand for
10 minutes, then stir well and serve.

thai chili beef burgers

Serves **4**
Preparation time **10 minutes**
Cooking time **10–12 minutes**

1 lb **ground beef**
1 tablespoon **Thai red curry paste**
½ cup **fresh white bread crumbs**
2 tablespoons chopped **cilantro**
1 **egg**, lightly beaten
1 tablespoon **light soy sauce**
black pepper

To serve
1 **baguette**, cut into 4 and split lengthwise
shredded lettuce
sweet chili sauce

Put the ground beef in a bowl and stir in the red curry paste, bread crumbs, cilantro, egg, soy sauce, and pepper. Mix together thoroughly with your hands until sticky. Shape the mixture into 8 mini burgers.

Heat a ridged griddle pan until very hot, add the burgers, and cook over a high heat for 4–5 minutes on each side until charred and cooked through.

Serve each burger in the baguettes with some shredded lettuce and sweet chili sauce.

For beef satay burgers, prepare and cook the burgers as above. Make a satay sauce by combining 6 tablespoons coconut cream, 3 tablespoons peanut sauce, juice of ½ lime, 2 teaspoons Thai fish sauce, and 2 teaspoons sweet chili sauce in a saucepan. Heat gently, stirring, for 2–3 minutes until blended. Assemble the burgers in toasted sesame seed buns with some salad leaves and the satay sauce.

shepherd's pie

Serves **4–6**
Preparation time **20 minutes**
Cooking time **1 hour**
   20 minutes–1 hour
   25 minutes

1 tablespoon **olive oil**
1 **onion**, finely chopped
1 **carrot**, diced
1 **celery stick**, diced
1 tablespoon chopped
   thyme
1 lb **ground lamb**
13 oz can **chopped
   tomatoes**
4 tablespoons **tomato paste**
1½ lb **boiling potatoes**,
   peeled and cubed
¼ cup **butter**
3 tablespoons **milk**
¾ cup grated **cheddar
   cheese**
salt and **black pepper**

Heat the oil in a saucepan, add the onion, carrot, celery, and thyme and cook gently for 10 minutes until soft and golden.

Add the ground lamb and cook over a high heat, breaking up with a wooden spoon, for 5 minutes until browned. Add the tomatoes, tomato paste, and salt and pepper to taste. Bring to a boil, then reduce the heat, cover, and simmer for 30 minutes.

Remove the lid and cook for an additional 15 minutes until thickened.

Meanwhile, put the potatoes in a large saucepan of lightly salted water and bring to a boil. Reduce the heat and simmer for 15–20 minutes until really tender. Drain well and return to the pan. Mash in the butter, milk, and half the cheese and season to taste with salt and pepper.

Spoon the ground lamb mixture into an 8 cup baking dish and carefully spoon the mash over the top, spreading over the surface of the filling. Fork the top of the mash and sprinkle with the remaining cheese. Bake in a preheated oven, 375°F, for 20–25 minutes until bubbling and golden.

For curried lamb phyllo pies, prepare and cook the ground meat mixture as above, adding 1 tablespoon medium curry paste with the tomatoes, tomato paste and seasoning. Spoon the filling into 6 x 1¼ cup ovenproof dishes. Layer 4 sheets of phyllo pastry together, brushing each with melted butter. Cut into 6 and scrunch each over a dish to cover. Bake in a preheated oven, 375°F, for 20 minutes.

chili tacos

Serves **4**
Preparation time **15 minutes**
Cooking time **25 minutes**

2 tablespoons **olive oil**
1 large **onion**, finely
 chopped
2 **garlic cloves**, crushed
1 lb **lean ground beef**
1 lb 7 oz jar **passata (sieved
 tomatoes)**
13 oz can **red kidney beans**,
 drained
2–3 tablespoon **hot chili
 sauce**
8 **soft corn tortillas**
1 cup grated **cheddar
 cheese**
½ cup **sour cream**
handful **fresh cilantro sprigs**
salt and **black pepper**

Heat the oil in a saucepan, add the onion and garlic, and cook over a high heat for 5 minutes.

Add the ground beef and cook, breaking it up with a wooden spoon, for 5 minutes until browned. Stir in the passata, beans, chili sauce, and salt and pepper to taste and bring to a boil. Reduce the heat and simmer, uncovered, for 15 minutes until thickened.

Meanwhile, put the corn tortillas on a large baking sheet and heat in a preheated oven, 350°F, for 5 minutes.

Serve the tortillas on a platter in the center of the table. Take 2 tortillas per person and spoon some chili into each one. Top with a quarter of the cheese and sour cream and a little cilantro, roll up, and serve.

For lentil & red pepper chili, heat 2 tablespoons olive oil in a saucepan, add 1 finely chopped large onion, 1 large cored, seeded, and chopped red bell pepper, and 2 crushed garlic cloves and cook over a high heat for 5 minutes. Add 2 x 13 oz cans brown lentils, drained, together with the passata, beans, chili sauce, and salt and pepper to taste as above. Bring to a boil, then reduce the heat and simmer, uncovered, for 15 minutes. Meanwhile, cook 1½ cups basmati rice in a large saucepan of salted boiling water for 10–12 minutes until just tender, then drain. Serve the chili hot with the rice, guacamole (see page 26 for homemade), and sour cream.

swordfish brochettes & lemon rice

Serves **4**
Preparation time **10 minutes**,
   plus standing
Cooking time **20 minutes**

3 tablespoons **extra virgin
   olive oil**
1 large **onion**, finely chopped
2 teaspoons **ground turmeric**
1 teaspoon **ground cinnamon**
grated **zest** and **juice** of
   1 **lemon**
1½ cups **jasmine rice**
3 cups **chicken stock** (see
   page 44 for homemade)
1½ lb **swordfish steaks**, cut
   into 1 inch dice
2 tablespoons chopped
   cilantro
salt and **black pepper**
spray oil for oiling

Heat 2 tablespoons of the oil in a saucepan, and add the onion, spices, lemon zest, and salt and pepper to taste and cook gently for 5 minutes until softened.

Add the rice and stir well. Pour in the stock and bring to a boil. Reduce the heat, cover, and simmer gently for 10 minutes. Stir in the lemon juice, remove the pan from the heat, and allow to stand, covered, for 10 minutes. Stir in the cilantro.

While the rice is standing, thread the swordfish cubes onto 8 bamboo skewers, presoaked in boiling water for 10 minutes. Brush with the remaining oil and season well with salt and pepper. Spray a preheated ridged griddle pan with oil and cook the brochettes for 2 minutes on each side until evenly browned. Serve the rice and kebabs with an arugula salad, if desired.

For shrimp, cranberry, & cashew nut pilaf, prepare and cook the rice as above. After simmering gently for 10 minutes, stir in the juice of the lemon with 12 oz cooked peeled shrimp, ⅓ cup toasted unsalted cashew nuts, and ½ cup dried cranberries. Allow to stand, covered, for 10 minutes before serving.

salmon with fennel & tomatoes

Serves **4**
Preparation time **10 minutes**
Cooking time **25 minutes**

4 **salmon fillets**, about
  6–8 oz each
4 tablespoons **lemon juice**
4 tablespoons **olive oil**
1 tablespoon **balsamic
  vinegar**
1 tablespoon **honey**
4 **garlic cloves**, finely
  chopped
2 **red onions**, quartered
2 **fennel bulbs**, quartered
16–20 **vine cherry tomatoes**
salt and **black pepper**

Season the salmon fillets generously with salt and
pepper and pour over the lemon juice. Set aside.

Combine the oil, vinegar, honey, garlic, and salt and
pepper to taste in a small bowl. Put the onions, fennel,
and tomatoes in a large bowl and pour over the oil
mixture. Toss to coat thoroughly, then spread out on a
baking sheet.

Roast in a preheated oven, 425°F, for 10 minutes. Add
the salmon fillets to the baking sheet and roast for an
additional 12–15 minutes.

Serve the salmon with the roasted vegetables and rice
or couscous.

For lemon & herb couscous to serve with the salmon
and fennel, put 1½ cups couscous in a heatproof bowl
and pour over 1 cup boiling vegetable stock (see
page 58 for homemade). Cover the bowl with a clean
dish towel and allow to stand for 5 minutes, or until
the grains are swollen and all the liquid has been
absorbed. Stir in 2 tablespoons extra virgin olive oil,
the juice of 1 lemon, and 2 tablespoons chopped
mixed herbs, fluffing up the grains with a fork.

tuna fish cakes

Serves **4**
Preparation time **10 minutes**
Cooking time **20 minutes**

2 x 14 oz cans **tuna in olive
  oil**, drained
1¼ cups **ricotta cheese**
6 **scallions**, finely chopped
grated **zest** and **juice** of
  1 **lime**
1 tablespoon chopped **dill
  weed**
1 **egg**, beaten
3 tablespoons **extra virgin
  olive oil**
2½ cups **baby arugula
  leaves**
salt and **black pepper**

Flake the tuna into a bowl and beat in the ricotta,
scallions, lime zest, dill, egg, and salt and pepper to taste
with a wooden spoon. Reserve 2 teaspoons of the lime
juice and beat the remainder into the tuna mixture.
Shape into 12 small cakes about 3 inches across.

Heat half the oil in a skillet, add the fish cakes,
in 2 batches, and cook over a medium heat for
4–5 minutes on each side until golden. Reduce the
heat if they start to over-brown and cook for 1 minute
more. Remove from the pan with a slotted spoon and
keep the cooked fish cakes warm in a preheated oven,
325°F, while you cook the remainder.

Meanwhile, beat the remaining oil and lime juice
together and toss with the arugula leaves in a bowl.
Serve the fish cakes with the arugula salad and some
garlic & herb mayonnaise (see below).

For quick garlic & herb mayonnaise to serve with
the fish cakes, add 1 crushed garlic clove, 2 teaspoons
lime juice, 1 tablespoon chopped fresh cilantro and a
pinch of cayenne pepper to ⅔ cup good-quality store-
bought mayonnaise in a bowl and mix well. Taste and
add more garlic according to taste.

warm scallop salad

Serves **4**
Preparation time **10 minutes**
Cooking time **3 minutes**

2 cups **wild strawberries**,
 hulled
2 tablespoons **balsamic
 vinegar**
1 tablespoon **lemon juice**,
 plus juice of **1 lemon**
3 tablespoons **olive oil**
1 2 **sea scallops**, without
 corals, cut into 3 slices
5 cups **mixed salad leaves**
salt and **black pepper**

To garnish
1 tablespoon **olive oil**
3 **leeks**, cut into matchstick-
 thin strips
20 **wild strawberries** or 8
 larger strawberries, sliced

Put the strawberries, vinegar, 1 tablespoon lemon juice, and oil in a food processor or blender and process until smooth. Pass through a fine sieve or cheesecloth to remove the seeds and set aside.

Season the scallops with salt and pepper and the remaining lemon juice.

Prepare the garnish. Heat the oil in a nonstick skillet, add the leeks, and cook over a high heat, stirring, for 1 minute, or until golden brown. Remove and set aside.

Add the scallop slices to the pan and cook for 20–30 seconds on each side. Divide the salad leaves into quarters and pile in the center of individual serving plates. Arrange the scallop slices over the salad.

Heat the strawberry mixture gently in a small saucepan for 20–30 seconds, then pour over the scallops and salad leaves. Sprinkle with the leeks and garnish with the strawberries. Sprinkle with a little pepper and serve.

For scallops with soy & honey dressing, beat together 2 tablespoons extra virgin olive oil, 1 teaspoon sesame oil, 1 tablespoon light soy sauce, 2 teaspoons balsamic vinegar, 1 teaspoon honey, and pepper to taste in a bowl. Cook the scallops as above (omitting the leeks) and arrange over the salad. Heat the dressing gently as above, then pour over the scallops and salad leaves.

fish 'n' oven fries

Serves **4**
Preparation time **10 minutes**
Cooking time **35–40 minutes**

4–6 large **potatoes**,
  scrubbed
2 tablespoons **olive oil**, plus
  extra for pan-frying
1 cup **dried bread crumbs**
⅓ cup **cornmeal**
1 tablespoon chopped
  thyme
4 **haddock** or **cod fillets**,
  about 6 oz each
3 tablespoons **all-purpose
  flour**, seasoned with salt
  and black pepper
2 **eggs**, lightly beaten
salt and **black pepper**
tomato ketchup, to serve

Cut the potatoes into wedges (you should get about 8–12 thick wedges from each potato). Toss with the oil and salt and pepper to taste in a roasting pan and roast in a preheated oven, 425°F, for 35–40 minutes, turning once, until evenly browned.

Meanwhile, combine the bread crumbs, cornmeal, thyme, and salt and pepper to taste in a large bowl. Dust each fish fillet with seasoned flour and then dip into the beaten egg and finally into the bread crumb mixture to completely coat the fish.

About 10 minutes before the fries are ready, heat ½ inch oil in a large skillet, add the fish fillets, in 2 batches, and cook over a medium heat for 2–3 minutes on each side until the coating is crisp and golden and the fish is cooked through. Remove from the pan with a spatula and keep warm in the bottom of the oven while you cook the remainder. Serve with the oven fries and tomato ketchup.

For crispy-coated chicken niblets, cut 2 skinless chicken breast fillets into strips about 1 inch thick. Following the method above, dip the chicken pieces into the seasoned flour, then the beaten egg and finally the bread crumb mixture to completely coat. Pan-fry as above, in 2 batches, for 4–5 minutes on each side until crisp and golden. Serve with Quick Garlic & Herb Mayonnaise (see page 158) for dipping.

prosciutto-wrapped salmon

Serves **4**
Preparation time **10 minutes**
Cooking time **10 minutes**

4 **salmon fillets**, about 6 oz
   each, skinned
4 thin slices of **fontina**
   cheese, rind removed
16 **sage leaves**
8 thin slices of **prosciutto**
salt and **black pepper**
arugula and parsley pasta,
   to serve (see below)

Season the salmon fillets with salt and pepper. Trim the slices of fontina to fit on top of the salmon.

Lay a slice of the trimmed cheese on top of each salmon fillet, followed by 4 sage leaves. Wrap 2 slices of prosciutto around each salmon fillet to hold the cheese and sage leaves in place.

Heat a griddle pan until hot, add the wrapped salmon fillets and cook for 5 minutes on each side, taking care when turning them over.

Serve the salmon hot with arugula and parsley pasta (see below).

For arugula & parsley pasta to serve as an accompaniment, plunge 12 oz dried fusilli into a large saucepan of lightly salted boiling water, return to a boil, and cook for 10–12 minutes until al dente. Drain well and return to the pan. Add 2 tablespoons extra virgin olive oil, 1¼ cups baby arugula leaves, 2 tablespoons torn flat-leaf parsley leaves, and salt and pepper to taste and stir well.

easy fish pie

Serves **4**
Preparation time **15 minutes**
Cooking time **40 minutes**

⅓ cup **butter**
1 small **onion**, finely chopped
1 **leek**, sliced
2 **celery sticks**, sliced
2 **garlic cloves**, crushed
grated **zest** of 1 **lemon**
2 teaspoons chopped
  tarragon
1¼ cups **heavy cream**
1 lb **white fish fillets**, such
  as haddock, cod, or
  flounder, cubed
5 oz **raw peeled shrimp**
1 small **baguette**, thinly
  sliced
salt and **black pepper**

Melt 2 tablespoons of the butter in a saucepan, add the onion, leek, celery, garlic, lemon zest, tarragon, and salt and pepper to taste and cook gently for 10 minutes until soft.

Add the cream and bring to a boil, then reduce the heat and simmer gently for 2 minutes until thickened. Remove from the heat and stir in the fish and shrimp.

Spoon the seafood mixture into a 4 cup pie dish. Melt the remaining butter in a small saucepan. Arrange the bread slices over the fish, overlapping, and brush with the melted butter.

Bake in a preheated oven, 350°F, for 15–20 minutes until the bread is golden. Cover with foil and bake for an additional 10 minutes until the fish is cooked.

For curried shrimp pies, after the onion and leek mixture has been cooked for 10 minutes as above, stir in 2 teaspoons mild curry powder and cook over a medium heat, stirring constantly, for 2 minutes. Add the cream and bring to a boil, then reduce the heat and simmer gently for 2 minutes until thickened. Remove the pan from the heat and stir in 1 cup thawed frozen peas with the fish and shrimp. Spoon the mixture into 4 individual baking dishes. Divide the bread slices between the dishes, brush with the melted butter, and bake in the oven as above for 15 minutes.

shrimp in chilied tomato sauce

Serves **4**
Preparation time **10 minutes**
Cooking time **10–12 minutes**

2 tablespoons **olive oil**
2 **red onions**, finely chopped
3 **garlic cloves**, crushed
1 **red chili**, seeded and
  chopped
2 strips of **lemon rind**
2 large **tomatoes**, seeded
  and chopped
⅓ cup **fish stock** (see below
  for homemade)
1 lb **raw peeled jumbo
  shrimp** (heads, tails, and
  shells reserved for making
  stock, optional)
salt and **black pepper**
2 tablespoons chopped
  mixed **parsley** and **dill
  weed**

Heat the oil in a heavy skillet, add the onions, garlic, chili, and lemon rind and cook over a medium heat, stirring, for 1–2 minutes.

Add the tomatoes and stock to the pan and bring to a boil, then reduce the heat and simmer for 5 minutes.

Add the shrimp, season to taste with salt and pepper, and cook, turning occasionally, for about 4 minutes, or until the shrimp turn pink.

Sprinkle with the mixed herbs and serve immediately.

For homemade fish stock, put the shrimp heads, tails, and shells in a mortar and lightly pound with a pestle. Put in a saucepan with the juice of ½ lemon and ⅔ cup dry white wine and bring to a boil. Add 5 cups water, 1 diced onion, 1 garlic clove, peeled but left whole, 3–4 parsley stalks, and 2–3 black peppercorns. Reduce the heat and simmer for about 15 minutes. Strain and use. This makes about 4 cups stock.

vegetarian dishes & salads

spring vegetable & herb pilaf

Serves **4**
Preparation time **10 minutes**,
plus standing
Cooking time **20 minutes**

2 tablespoons **extra virgin
olive oil**
1 **leek**, sliced
1 **zucchini**, diced
grated **zest** and **juice** of
1 **lemon**
2 **garlic cloves**, crushed
1½ cups **long-grain rice**
2½ cups hot **vegetable stock**
(see page 58 for
homemade)
1 cup **green beans**, chopped
1 cup **fresh** or **frozen peas**
4 tablespoons chopped
mixed herbs, such as mint,
parsley, and chives
½ cup **slivered almonds**,
toasted
salt and **black pepper**

Heat the oil in a large skillet, add the leek, zucchini, lemon zest, garlic, and a little salt and pepper and cook gently over a medium-low heat for 5 minutes.

Add the rice, stir once, and pour in the hot stock. Bring to a boil, then reduce the heat, cover, and simmer gently for 10 minutes.

Stir in the beans and peas, cover, and cook for an additional 5 minutes.

Remove the pan from the heat and allow to stand for 5 minutes. Stir in the lemon juice and herbs and serve scattered with the slivered almonds.

For winter vegetable & fruit pilaf, heat 2 tablespoons extra virgin olive oil in a large skillet, add 1 sliced red onion, 1 teaspoon ground coriander, and 2 teaspoons chopped thyme and cook gently over a medium-low heat for 5 minutes. Add 3 cups diced pumpkin flesh with the rice as above, stir once, and pour in the hot stock. Bring to a boil, then reduce the heat, cover, and simmer gently for 10 minutes. Stir in ½ cup raisins with the peas as above, cover, and cook for 5 minutes. Remove the pan from the heat and allow to stand for 5 minutes. Stir in 2 tablespoons chopped fresh cilantro with the lemon juice and almonds.

spaghetti with easy tomato sauce

Serves **4**
Preparation time **5 minutes**
Cooking time **30 minutes**

13 oz **dried spaghetti**
salt and **black pepper**
¼ cup freshly grated
   Parmesan cheese, to serve

Easy tomato sauce
2 x 13 oz cans **chopped
   tomatoes**
2 tablespoons **extra virgin
   olive oil**
2 large **garlic cloves**,
   crushed
1 teaspoon **superfine sugar**
¼ teaspoon **dried red
   pepper flakes**
2 tablespoons chopped
   fresh basil

Start by making the sauce. Place the tomatoes, oil, garlic, sugar, pepper flakes, and some salt and pepper in a saucepan and bring to a boil. Lower the heat and simmer gently for 20–30 minutes until thickened and full of flavor.

Stir in the basil and adjust the seasoning. Keep warm.

Meanwhile, plunge the pasta into a saucepan of lightly salted, boiling water, bring back to a boil, and cook for 10–12 minutes or until just tender. Drain the pasta and divide between bowls, spoon over the sauce, and serve with Parmesan cheese.

For a spicy tomato & olive sauce, follow the recipe above but adding ½ teaspoon dried red pepper flakes. Stir in ⅔ cup pitted black olives just before the end of cooking and heat through.

eggplant & mozzarella bake

Serves **4**

Preparation time **15 minutes**,
plus making the sauce

Cooking time **25–30 minutes**

spray olive oil, for oiling

2 large **eggplants**, about
1 lb each

3 tablespoons **extra virgin
olive oil**

1 recipe quantity **Easy
Tomato Sauce** (see page
106)

2 cups grated **mozzarella
cheese**

¼ cup freshly grated
Parmesan cheese

Spray an 8 x 12 inch baking dish lightly with spray oil.
Cut the eggplants into thin slices, brush the slices with
the oil, and season with a little salt and pepper. Cook
under a preheated high broiler for 2–3 minutes on
each side until charred and softened.

Layer the eggplant slices, tomato sauce, and
mozzarella in the prepared baking dish to give
3 layers of each, ending with the mozzarella.
Sprinkle with the Parmesan.

Bake in a preheated oven, 400°F, for 20–25 minutes
until bubbling and golden. Serve with a crisp green
salad and some crusty bread.

For eggplant & mozzarella cannelloni, prepare the
eggplants and cook under a broiler as above. Cut the
mozzarella into cubes and roll each slice of eggplant
up with a cube of mozzarella and a basil leaf inside
to form the cannelloni. Place in the oiled baking dish,
pour over the tomato sauce, and sprinkle with an
extra ¾ cup grated mozzarella and the grated
Parmesan. Bake as above.

mixed vegetable curry

Serves **4** as a main dish or
6 as a side dish
Preparation time **15 minutes**
Cooking time **20–30 minutes**

2–3 tablespoons **vegetable
oil**
1 small **onion**, chopped, or
2 teaspoons **cumin seeds**
1 lb **mixed vegetables**, such
as potatoes, carrots,
rutabaga, peas, green
beans, and cauliflower, cut
into chunks or broken into
florets (green beans can
be left whole)
about 1 teaspoon **chili
powder**
2 teaspoons **ground coriander**
½ teaspoon **ground turmeric**
2–3 **tomatoes**, skinned and
chopped, or **juice** of
1 **lemon**
1¼ cups **water** (optional)
salt

Heat the oil in a heavy saucepan, add the onion, and
cook over a medium heat, stirring occasionally,
for about 10 minutes, or until golden. Alternatively,
add the cumin seeds and cook, stirring frequently,
until they sizzle.

Add the vegetables, chili powder, coriander, turmeric,
and salt to taste and cook, stirring constantly, for
2–3 minutes.

Stir in the tomatoes or the lemon juice. If a dry vegetable
curry is preferred, add only a little water, cover and cook
gently for 10–12 minutes until dry. For a more moist
curry, stir in the measurement water, cover, and simmer
for 5–6 minutes until the vegetables are tender.

Serve as a main dish with naan, chappatis, or basmati
rice, or on its own as a side dish.

For buttery spiced pita bread to serve as an
accompaniment, lay 4 large, round pita breads on
a baking sheet and warm through in a preheated
oven, 350°F, for 10 minutes. Meanwhile, put ½ cup
butter, 1 crushed garlic clove, ½ teaspoon ground
coriander, and a pinch of cayenne pepper in a
saucepan and cook gently for 3–4 minutes until
the garlic is soft and golden. Remove the pita bread
from the oven and brush the spiced butter mixture
all over each one.

chickpea tagine

Serves **4**
Preparation time **15 minutes**
Cooking time **40 minutes**

6 tablespoons **extra virgin
  olive oil**
1 large **onion**, finely chopped
2 **garlic cloves**, crushed
2 teaspoons **ground coriander**
1 teaspoon each **ground
  cumin, ground turmeric,**
  and **ground cinnamon**
1 large **eggplant**, about
  12 oz, diced
13 oz can **chickpeas**, drained
13 oz can chopped
  tomatoes
1¼ cups **vegetable stock**
  (see page 58 for
  homemade)
8 oz **button mushrooms**
½ cup chopped **dried figs**
2 tablespoons chopped
  cilantro
salt and **black pepper**
preserved lemon, chopped,
  to serve

Heat 2 tablespoons of the oil in a saucepan, add the onion, garlic, and spices and cook over a medium heat, stirring frequently, for 5 minutes until lightly golden.

Heat another 2 tablespoons of the oil in the pan, add the eggplants, and cook, stirring, for 4–5 minutes until browned. Add the chickpeas, tomatoes, and stock and bring to a boil. Reduce the heat, cover, and simmer gently for 20 minutes.

Meanwhile, heat the remaining oil in a skillet, add the mushrooms, and cook over a medium heat for 4–5 minutes until browned.

Add the mushrooms to the tagine with the figs and cook for an additional 10 minutes. Stir in the cilantro. Garnish with chopped preserved lemon and serve with couscous (see below).

For buttered couscous to serve as an accompaniment, put 1½ cups couscous in a heatproof bowl and pour over 1 cup boiling vegetable stock. Cover the bowl with a clean dish towel and allow to stand for 5 minutes, or until the grains are swollen and all the liquid has been absorbed. Add ¼ cup diced softened butter and gently fork through the grains to separate.

ratatouille

Serves **8**
Preparation time **10 minutes**
Cooking time **30 minutes**

½ cup **olive oil**
2 large **eggplants**, quartered
  lengthwise and cut into
  ½ inch slices
2 **zucchini**, cut into
  ½ inch slices
2 large **red bell peppers**,
  cored, seeded, and cut
  into squares
1 large **yellow bell pepper**,
  cored, seeded, and cut
  into squares
2 large **onions**, thinly sliced
3 large **garlic cloves**, crushed
2 tablespoons **tomato paste**
13 oz can **plum tomatoes**
12 **basil leaves**, chopped
1 tablespoon finely chopped
  marjoram or **oregano**
1 teaspoon finely chopped
  thyme
1 tablespoon **paprika**
2–4 tablespoons finely
  chopped **parsley**
salt and **black pepper**

Heat half the oil in a roasting pan in a preheated oven, 425°F. Add the eggplants, zucchini, and peppers and toss in the hot oil. Return to the oven and roast for about 30 minutes, or until tender.

Meanwhile, heat the remaining oil in a deep saucepan, add the onions and garlic and cook over a medium heat for 3–5 minutes until softened but not browned. Add the tomato paste, plum tomatoes, herbs, and paprika and season to taste with salt and pepper. Stir to combine, then cook for 10–15 minutes until the mixture is thick and syrupy.

Using a slotted spoon, transfer the vegetables from the roasting pan to the tomato mixture. Gently stir to combine, then add the parsley and adjust seasoning if necessary. Serve hot or cold with crusty bread or as an accompaniment to meats or poultry.

For ratatouille tartlets, using a 3 inch pastry cutter, stamp out 16 rounds from each of 2 x 12 inch sheets of thawed frozen shortcrust pastry. Press into 2 muffin pans. Prick the bases with a fork and chill in the refrigerator for 30 minutes. Meanwhile, prepare the ratatouille as above, but make only half the quantity. Bake the shells in a preheated oven, 400°F, for 10–12 minutes until golden. Spoon a little of the hot ratatouille into each shell, sprinkle with ¼ cup grated Parmesan cheese and serve as a starter.

halloumi & fig pastry pizza

Serves **2**
Preparation time **10 minutes**
Cooking time **25 minutes**

1 sheet of **frozen puff pastry**,
  10 inches square, thawed
3 tablespoons **green pesto**
  (see page 128 for
  homemade)
4 **fresh figs**, quartered
7 oz **halloumi cheese**,
  thinly sliced
⅔ cup **pitted black olives**,
  halved
2 tablespoons freshly grated
  Parmesan cheese
a few **mint leaves**, to garnish
salt and **black pepper**

Lay the pastry on a baking sheet and score a ½ inch border around the edge. Prick the base with a fork and spread the center with the pesto.

Arrange the figs, halloumi, and olives over the pesto and sprinkle with the Parmesan.

Place the baking sheet on another preheated baking sheet (this will ensure the pastry is crispy) and bake in a preheated oven, 400°F, for 10 minutes. Reduce the temperature to 325°F, and bake for an additional 15 minutes until the base is crispy. Sprinkle the mint leaves over to garnish and serve with an arugula salad.

For mini puff pastries, use a 2 inch pastry cutter to stamp out rounds from the pastry sheet. Top each with a spoonful of olive tapenade and a slice of fresh fig, then divide 5 oz crumbled goat cheese between the rounds. Sprinkle with the Parmesan and bake as above for 8–10 minutes. Serve warm.

layered cheese & tomato soufflé

Serves **4**

Preparation time **15 minutes**, plus cooling

Cooking time **45–50 minutes**

2 tablespoons **butter**, plus extra for greasing

1 **garlic clove**, crushed

1 small **onion**, chopped

12 oz **tomatoes**, skinned and chopped

2 teaspoons **dried oregano**

6–8 **pitted black olives**, chopped

salt and **black pepper**

Soufflé mixture

3 tablespoons **butter**

6 tablespoons **all-purpose flour**

1¼ cups **light cream** or **milk**

3 large **eggs**, separated

⅔ cup **full-fat cream cheese with garlic and herbs**, crumbled

Melt the butter in a heavy saucepan, add the garlic, onion, and tomatoes, and cook over a low heat, stirring occasionally, for 3–4 minutes. Add the oregano and olives and season to taste with salt and pepper. Remove the pan from the heat and allow to cool.

Meanwhile, for the soufflé, melt the butter in a saucepan, add the flour, and cook, stirring constantly, for 1 minute. Remove the pan from the heat and gradually add the cream or milk, stirring vigorously after each addition to ensure that it is fully incorporated. Return the pan to the heat and bring to a boil, stirring constantly, until thickened. Remove from the heat and beat in the egg yolks, 1 at a time. Add the cheese and stir until it has completely melted. Remove from the heat and allow to cool.

Beat the egg whites in a large bowl until just stiff enough to stand in peaks. Mix about 2 tablespoons of the egg whites into the cheese mixture, then carefully fold in the remaining egg whites with a metal spoon.

Grease a 6 cup soufflé dish and place it on a baking sheet. Spread the cooled tomato mixture in the dish and cover with the soufflé mixture. Bake immediately in a preheated oven, 375°F, for 35–40 minutes until well risen and golden brown. Serve immediately.

spinach & cheese quiche

Serves **4**
Preparation time **10 minutes**
Cooking time **25 minutes**

¼ cup **butter**
1 small **onion**, finely
  chopped
1 **garlic clove**, crushed
2 teaspoons chopped **thyme**
1¼ cups **frozen leaf spinach**,
  thawed
⅔ cup **light cream**
2 **eggs**, beaten
¼ cup freshly grated
  Parmesan cheese
8 inch **frozen pastry tart
  shell** (cook from frozen)
salt and **black pepper**

Melt the butter in a large skillet, add the onion, garlic, thyme, and salt and pepper to taste, and cook for 5 minutes. Squeeze out all the excess water from the spinach, add to the pan, and cook, stirring, for 2–3 minutes until heated through.

Beat together the cream, eggs, cheese, and a pinch of salt and pepper in a bowl. Spoon the spinach mixture into the tart shell, carefully pour over the cream mixture, and bake on a preheated baking sheet in a preheated oven, 400°F, for 20 minutes until set. Serve with a green salad.

For mushroom & sour cream tart, cook the onion, garlic, and thyme in the butter as above, then add 12 oz halved button mushrooms to the pan and cook until browned. Omit the spinach and continue as above, but replace the light cream with ⅔ cup sour cream.

baked cheese fondue

Serves **4**
Preparation time **5 minutes**
Cooking time **12–15 minutes**

1 whole **Camembert cheese**,
    about 7 oz
1 tablespoon **extra virgin
    olive oil**
1 tablespoon **honey**
2 teaspoons chopped **thyme
    leaves**, plus a few extra to
    garnish
1 **baguette**, sliced
8 oz **vine cherry tomatoes**
1 **dessert apple** or **pear**, cut
    into wedges
salt and **black pepper**

Put the Camembert on a baking sheet lined with foil.
Drizzle over the oil and honey and sprinkle with the
thyme and salt and pepper to taste.

Bake in a preheated oven, 400°F, for 12–15 minutes
until the cheese is sizzling and ready to burst through
the skin.

Carefully transfer to a platter and serve with the bread,
tomatoes, and fruit to dip into the oozing cheese.

For a fruit & nut baked cheese fondue, prepare and
bake the cheese as above, then top with 2 quartered
fresh figs and 2 tablespoons toasted and roughly
chopped pecan nuts.

cheesy pasta & mushroom bake

Serves **4**
Preparation time **10 minutes**
Cooking time **35–40 minutes**

spray olive oil, for oiling
3 tablespoons **extra virgin olive oil**
1 **onion**, finely chopped
2 **garlic cloves**, crushed
2 teaspoons chopped **sage**
8 oz **button mushrooms**, quartered
2½ cups **cheese sauce** (see below for homemade)
12 oz **dried penne**
2 tablespoons chopped **parsley**
4 tablespoons freshly grated **Parmesan cheese**
salt and **black pepper**

Spray 4 x 1¼ cup baking dishes lightly with spray oil. Heat 1 tablespoon of the olive oil in a skillet, add the onion, garlic, sage, and salt and pepper to taste and cook gently for 10 minutes until softened. Add the remaining oil, then increase the heat to high, add the mushrooms, and cook, stirring, for 3–4 minutes until golden.

Add the cheese sauce and heat gently for 2–3 minutes until just bubbling.

Meanwhile, plunge the pasta into a large saucepan of lightly salted boiling water. Return to a boil and cook for 10–12 minutes or until al dente. Drain well and return to the pan.

Stir the sauce into the pasta with the parsley and season to taste with salt and pepper.

Spoon the pasta into the prepared dish and sprinkle with the Parmesan. Bake in a preheated oven, 375°F, for 15–20 minutes until bubbling and golden. Serve with a crisp green salad.

For homemade cheese sauce, melt ¼ cup unsalted butter in a saucepan and stir in ½ cup all-purpose flour. Cook over a low heat, stirring, for 1 minute until golden. Gradually beat in 2½ cups milk and cook, stirring constantly, until the sauce is smooth. Bring to a boil, stirring, then reduce the heat and simmer for 2 minutes. Add salt and pepper to taste and remove the pan from the heat. Immediately stir in 1 cup grated cheddar cheese.

chestnut risotto cakes

Serves **4**
Preparation time **10 minutes**, plus soaking
Cooking time **20 minutes**

⅓ cup **dried porcini mushrooms**
1 tablespoon **olive oil**
¾ cup **risotto rice**
2½ cups hot **vegetable stock** (see page 58 for homemade)
¼ cup **butter**
1 **onion**, chopped
3 **garlic cloves**, crushed
1½ cups **cooked peeled chestnuts**, chopped
¾ cup freshly grated **Parmesan cheese**
1 **egg**, lightly beaten
⅓ cup **cornmeal**
vegetable oil, for pan-frying
salt and **black pepper**
lemon wedges, to garnish

Put the dried mushrooms in a heatproof bowl and cover with boiling water. Allow to soak while you prepare the rice.

Heat the olive oil in a heavy saucepan, add the rice, and stir well to coat the grains with the oil. Add the hot stock and bring to a boil. Reduce the heat, partially cover, and simmer, stirring frequently, for 12–15 minutes until the rice is tender and all the stock has been absorbed. Transfer to a bowl.

Meanwhile, melt the butter in a saucepan, add the onion and garlic, and cook gently for 5 minutes.

Drain and chop the soaked mushrooms, then add to the rice with the onion mixture, chestnuts, Parmesan, and egg. Stir until well combined and season to taste with salt and pepper.

Divide the mixture into 12 portions. Pat each portion into a cake and roll in the cornmeal. Heat a shallow depth of vegetable oil in a skillet, add the cakes and cook for 2 minutes on each side until golden. Garnish each serving with a lemon wedge and serve immediately with mixed salad leaves.

roasted vegetable & herb couscous

Serves **6**
Preparation time **15 minutes**,
  plus soaking
Cooking time **25 minutes**

4 cups diced **pumpkin**
4 **zucchini**, diced
1 **red onion**, cut into wedges
⅓ cup **extra virgin olive oil**
1 cup **couscous**
1 cup **boiling water**
8 oz **cherry tomatoes**, halved
2 tablespoons each
  chopped **cilantro**, **mint**,
  and **parsley**
juice of 1 large **lemon**
salt and **black pepper**

Put the pumpkin, zucchini, and onion in a roasting pan with 2 tablespoons of the oil, season to taste with salt and pepper, and stir to combine.

Roast in a preheated oven, 425°F, for 25 minutes until all the vegetables are cooked.

Meanwhile, put the couscous in a heatproof bowl and pour over the measurement boiling water. Cover the bowl with a clean dish towel and allow to stand for 5 minutes, or until the grains are swollen and all the liquid has been absorbed.

Fork through the couscous to fluff up the grains, then stir in the roasted vegetables, cherry tomatoes, and herbs.

Beat together the remaining oil, the lemon juice, and salt and pepper to taste in a small bowl and stir through the salad.

For vegetable kebabs with herb couscous, cut 4 zucchini into chunks and 1 red onion into wedges. Core and seed 1 red bell pepper and cut into chunks. Thread the vegetables onto metal skewers, interspersed with 16 button mushrooms, brush with olive oil, and season to taste with salt and pepper. Cook under a preheated high broiler for 8–10 minutes, turning halfway through, until charred and cooked through. Make the couscous as above and serve with the kebabs.

bean, goat cheese, & nut salad

Serves **4**
Preparation time **10 minutes**
Cooking time **3 minutes**

1 lb fine **green beans**
5 oz **goat cheese**, crumbled
1 cup **pecan nuts**, toasted
2½ cups **baby arugula**
  leaves
1 large handful **flat-leaf**
  parsley leaves

Dressing
3 tablespoons **walnut oil**
1 tablespoon **extra virgin**
  olive oil
1 tablespoon **sherry vinegar**
1 teaspoon **superfine sugar**
1 small **garlic clove**, crushed
salt and **black pepper**

Cook the beans in a saucepan of lightly salted boiling water for 3 minutes.

Drain the beans well and refresh under cold water. Drain again and pat dry. Put in a bowl with the goat cheese, pecan nuts, arugula, and parsley.

Make the dressing. Beat the ingredients together in a small bowl. Add to the salad, toss well, and serve.

For bean & nut salad with goat cheese dressing, prepare the salad as above but omit the goat cheese. Put 4 oz crumbled goat cheese in a bowl and beat in 1 tablespoon raspberry wine vinegar, 2 teaspoons honey, ½ cup extra virgin olive oil, 2 tablespoons boiling water, and salt and pepper to taste. Drizzle over the salad and serve.

warm lentil & goat cheese salad

Serves **4**
Preparation time **10 minutes**
Cooking time **20–30 minutes**

2 teaspoons **olive oil**
2 teaspoons **cumin seeds**
2 **garlic cloves**, crushed
2 teaspoons grated **fresh ginger root**
½ cup **Puy lentils**
3 cups **vegetable stock** (see page 58 for homemade)
2 tablespoons chopped **mint**
2 tablespoons chopped **cilantro**
½ **lime**
3 cups **baby spinach leaves**
4 oz **goat cheese**, crumbled
black pepper

Heat the oil in a saucepan, add the cumin seeds, garlic, and ginger and cook over a medium heat, stirring, for 1 minute.

Add the lentils and cook for an additional minute.

Add the stock, a large ladleful at a time, and cook until each addition has been absorbed before adding the next. Continue in this way until all the stock has been absorbed. This should take about 20–30 minutes. Remove from the heat and stir in the mint and cilantro with a squeeze of lime juice.

To serve, divide the spinach leaves between individual bowls, top with a quarter of the lentils and the goat cheese, and sprinkle with pepper.

For lentil salad with grilled halloumi, prepare the lentil salad as above, but omit the goat cheese and replace the spinach leaves with 3 cups arugula leaves. Cut 8 oz halloumi cheese into 8 slices. Heat a nonstick skillet until hot, add the cheese slices, and cook over a high heat for 1 minute on each side until charred and softened. Arrange the halloumi slices over the salad, squeeze over the juice from ½ lemon, and drizzle over a little extra virgin olive oil.

roasted sweet potato salad

Serves **4**

Preparation time **15 minutes**, plus cooling

Cooking time **30–35 minutes**

1 lb **sweet potatoes**, peeled and cubed

2 tablespoons **extra virgin olive oil**

1 teaspoon **ground coriander**

½ teaspoon **ground cumin**

¼ teaspoon **ground cinnamon**

6 oz **green beans**

3 cups **baby spinach leaves**

½ cup **shelled pistachio nuts**, toasted

salt and **black pepper**

Dressing

2 tablespoons **plain yogurt**

1 small **garlic clove**, crushed

1 large **red chili**, seeded and finely chopped

1 tablespoon **lemon juice**

1 teaspoon **honey**

3 tablespoons **extra virgin olive oil**

Put the sweet potatoes in a roasting pan. Combine the oil, spices, and salt and pepper to taste in a small bowl, pour over the potatoes, and stir well to evenly coat.

Roast in a preheated oven, 425°F, for 30–35 minutes, stirring halfway through, until golden and tender. Allow to cool for 30 minutes.

Meanwhile, blanch the beans in a saucepan of lightly salted boiling water for 2–3 minutes until just tender. Drain and refresh under cold water. Drain again and pat dry.

Put the beans in a large bowl with the cooled sweet potatoes, spinach leaves, and pistachio nuts.

Make the dressing. Mix together the yogurt, garlic, chili, lemon juice, honey, and salt and pepper to taste in a bowl. Beat in the oil until evenly blended. Pour over the salad, stir well, and serve.

For sesame and soy dressing as an alternative for the salad, beat together 2 tablespoons olive oil, 2 teaspoons sesame oil, 1 tablespoon light soy sauce, 1 teaspoon honey, and a little pepper in a small bowl. Prepare the salad as above and serve drizzled with the dressing, garnished with 2 tablespoons toasted sesame seeds.

easy
desserts
& cakes

lemon creams with raspberries

Serves **4**
Preparation time **5 minutes**,
  plus chilling & standing
Cooking time **5 minutes**

1¾ cups **heavy cream**
½ cup **superfine sugar**
6 tablespoons **lemon juice**
1¼ cups **fresh raspberries**
2 tablespoons **confectioners'
  sugar**

Heat the cream and superfine sugar together in a saucepan until the sugar has dissolved. Bring to a boil, then reduce the heat and simmer for 3 minutes.

Remove the pan from the heat, add the lemon juice, and immediately pour into ⅔ cup ramekins. Set aside to cool completely, then chill overnight in the refrigerator.

Combine the raspberries and confectioners' sugar in a bowl and mash lightly. Allow to stand for 30 minutes until really juicy. Spoon the raspberry mixture onto the lemon creams and serve with crispy cinnamon cookies (see below).

For crispy cinnamon cookies to serve as an accompaniment, spray 2 baking sheets lightly with spray olive oil. Put 1 cup softened unsalted butter, ½ cup superfine sugar, 1 tablespoon milk, 2½ cups self-rising flour, and 1 teaspoon ground cinnamon in a food processor and process until smooth. Roll small pieces of the dough into balls and flatten into 2 inch discs. Place on the prepared baking sheets and bake in a preheated oven, 350°F, for 12–15 minutes until lightly golden. Allow to cool on the baking sheets for 5 minutes, then transfer to a cooling rack to cool completely.

sticky toffee puddings

Serves **4**
Preparation time **10 minutes**
Cooking time **25–30 minutes**

spray olive oil, for oiling
2 tablespoons **corn syrup**
2 tablespoons **molasses**
⅔ cup **butter**, softened
2 tablespoons **heavy cream**
½ cup **superfine sugar**
2 **eggs**, beaten
1 cup **self-rising flour**
½ cup **walnuts**, lightly toasted
   and ground

Spray 4 x ¾ cup ramekins lightly with spray oil. In a small saucepan, heat together the corn syrup, molasses, and ¼ cup of the butter until melted. Divide half the mixture between the prepared ramekins, stir the cream into the remainder and set aside.

Put the remaining butter and sugar in a food processor and process briefly. Add the eggs and flour and process again for 30 seconds. Stir in the walnuts.

Spoon the batter into the ramekins to cover the syrup mixture.

Stand the ramekins in a shallow roasting pan and bake in a preheated oven, 350°F, for 25–30 minutes until risen and golden.

Remove the ramekins from the oven and allow to stand for 5 minutes. Meanwhile, heat the remaining syrup mixture. Unmold the puddings and pour over the syrup. Serve with custard (see page 218 for homemade) or clotted cream.

For sticky date & orange puddings, prepare the corn syrup mixture, dividing half the mixture between ramekins and stirring cream into the remainder as above. Process the remaining butter and sugar, then add the eggs and flour as above. Fold in ½ cup finely chopped dates, grated zest of 1 orange, and ¼ cup ground pecan nuts. Spoon over the syrup mixture and bake as above. Serve with the warmed syrup as above.

summer pudding

Serves **8**
Preparation time **15 minutes**,
    plus chilling
Cooking time **10–15 minutes**

2¼ cups **fresh** or **frozen red
    currants**, thawed if frozen,
    plus extra sprigs to
    decorate (optional)
½ cup **superfine sugar**
1⅔ cup **fresh** or **frozen
    strawberries**, thawed
    if frozen
2 cups **fresh** or **frozen
    raspberries**, thawed
    if frozen
8 slices of **white bread**,
    crusts removed

Put the red currants and sugar in a heavy saucepan
and cook over a low heat, stirring occasionally, for 10–
15 minutes until tender. Add the strawberries and
raspberries, remove from the heat, and allow to cool.
Strain the fruit, reserving the juice.

Cut 3 rounds of bread the same diameter as a 3¾ cup
pudding basin. Shape the remaining bread to fit around
the side of the basin. Soak all the bread in the reserved
fruit juice.

Line the base of the basin with one of the rounds,
then arrange the shaped bread around the side. Pour
in half the fruit and place another round of bread on
top. Cover with the remaining fruit, then top with the
remaining bread round.

Cover with a saucer small enough to fit inside the
basin and put a 1 lb weight on top or weigh down
with food cans. Chill in the refrigerator overnight.

Turn out onto a serving plate, pour over any remaining
fruit juice, and decorate with a few red currant sprigs
arranged on top of the pudding in the center, if desired.
Serve with whipped or pouring cream.

chocolate & raspberry pudding

Serves **6**
Preparation time **15 minutes**
Cooking time **40–45 minutes**

olive oil spray, for oiling
1½ cups **fresh raspberries**
1 cup **self-rising flour**
⅓ cup **cocoa powder**
½ cup **superfine sugar**
1 cup **milk**
⅓ cup **unsalted butter**,
    melted
2 **eggs**, beaten

Topping
⅓ cup **superfine sugar**
⅓ cup **light brown sugar**
2 tablespoons **cocoa
    powder**
1½ cups **boiling water**
confectioners' sugar,
    for dusting

Spray a 4 cup baking dish lightly with spray oil. Sprinkle the raspberries over the base of the dish.

Sift the flour and cocoa powder into a bowl and stir in the superfine sugar. Make a well in the center and beat in the milk, melted butter, and eggs to form a smooth batter (it should be quite runny). Pour the mixture into the dish, covering the raspberries.

Make the topping. Combine the sugars and cocoa powder and sprinkle over the top of the chocolate mixture. Very carefully pour the measurement boiling water over the top as evenly as possible.

Bake in a preheated oven, 350°F, for 40–45 minutes until the pudding is firm to the touch and some "bubbles" of sauce appear on the top. Rest for 5 minutes, then dust with confectioners' sugar and serve.

For chocolate & orange pudding, make the chocolate pudding mixture as above, but omit the raspberries. Pour the mixture into the baking dish. For the topping, combine the sugars and cocoa powder and sprinkle over the pudding mixture as above. Pour 1½ cups orange juice into a saucepan and heat until boiling point. Stir in 2 tablespoons of Cointreau or brandy. Pour over the top of the pudding mixture. Bake in the oven as above, dust with confectioners' sugar, and serve with whipped cream.

venetian rice pudding

Serves **4**
Preparation time **10 minutes**,
  plus soaking
Cooking time **20–30 minutes**

½ cup **golden raisins**
3 tablespoons **medium sherry**
  (optional)
2½ cups hot **lowfat milk**
⅔ cup **heavy cream**
1 **vanilla bean**, split
  lengthwise, or 2 teaspoons
  vanilla extract
¼ cup **superfine sugar**
½ teaspoon **ground mixed**
  spice
grated **zest** of 1 lemon
½ cup **risotto rice**
strips of **lemon rind**, to
  decorate

Put the golden raisins in a bowl with the sherry, if using, and allow to soak while you prepare the risotto.

Put milk, cream, vanilla bean or extract, sugar, mixed spice, and grated lemon zest in a saucepan and bring almost to a boil.

Add the rice to the pan and cook on the lowest heat, stirring frequently, for 20–30 minutes, or until the rice is creamy but the grains are still firm.

Stir in the golden raisins and any sherry from the bowl and serve warm or cold, decorated with lemon rind strips.

For coconut rice pudding with mango, put ¾ cup short-grain rice, 4 cups coconut milk, and ¼ cup superfine sugar in a saucepan. Bring to a boil, then reduce the heat and cook gently, stirring occasionally, for 25–30 minutes until the milk has been absorbed and the rice is tender. Spoon into bowls and serve topped with 1 peeled, pitted, and sliced mango and a drizzle of honey.

granola berry crumble

Serves **4**
Preparation time **10 minutes**
Cooking time **20 minutes**

spray olive oil, for oiling
1⅓ cups **fresh blueberries**
1 cup **fresh strawberries**,
  hulled and halved
2 **peaches**, quartered, pitted,
  and sliced
4 tablespoons **orange juice**
2 tablespoons **light brown
  sugar**
2 tablespoons **butter**, diced
2½ cups **good-quality
  granola**
1 tablespoon **all-purpose
  flour**
4 tablespoons **light cream**,
  plus extra to serve

Spray 4 x 1 cup ramekins lightly with spray oil.
Combine the berries, peaches, orange juice, and sugar
in a bowl, then divide between the prepared ramekins.
Add half the butter to the ramekins.

Put the granola in a bowl, add the flour and cream, and
stir until all the granola is moistened. Sprinkle over the
top of the fruit mixture in the ramekins and add the
remaining butter.

Stand the ramekins in a shallow roasting pan and
bake in a preheated oven, 350°F, for 20 minutes until
the topping is golden and the fruit bubbling. Serve
with cream.

For apple & blackberry crumble, put 1 lb peeled
and diced apples and ¾ cup fresh or frozen
blackberries in a saucepan with 2 tablespoons
superfine sugar, 2 tablespoons butter, 1 teaspoon
ground cinnamon, and 4 tablespoons water. Warm
through for 5 minutes until the butter is melted and
the fruit softened. Divide between the oiled ramekins,
add the granola topping, and bake as above. Serve
with custard (see page 218 for homemade).

freeform apple tart

Serves **6**
Preparation time **10 minutes**
Cooking time **20–25 minutes**

1 large sheet of **shortcrust
   pastry**, 12 inches square,
   thawed if frozen
1 lb **Granny Smith apples**,
   peeled, cored, and
   thinly sliced
⅓ cup **raisins**
2 tablespoons **light brown
   sugar**
2 tablespoons **butter**, melted
½ teaspoon **ground
   cinnamon**
1 tablespoon **milk**
1 tablespoon **confectioners'
   sugar**, plus extra to serve

Lay the pastry sheet on a baking sheet lined with
parchment paper and trim each corner to make a
roughly round piece of pastry.

Mix together the apples, raisins, brown sugar, melted
butter, and cinnamon in a bowl until evenly combined.
Spoon the apple mixture onto the pastry sheet,
arranging it in a circle, leaving a 1 inch border. Pull
the pastry edges up and over the filling to make a rim.
Brush the pastry with the milk and dust with the
confectioners' sugar.

Bake in a preheated oven, 350°F, for 20–25 minutes
until the pastry is golden and the fruit softened. Dust
with extra confectioners' sugar and serve warm with
custard (see below).

For homemade custard to serve as an accompaniment,
put 2½ cups milk and 1 vanilla bean, split lengthwise,
in a saucepan and heat gently until it reaches boiling
point. Remove from the heat and allow to infuse for
15 minutes. Remove the vanilla bean. Beat 6 egg yolks
and 2 tablespoons superfine sugar together in a bowl
until pale and creamy, then stir in the infused milk.
Return to the pan and cook, stirring constantly, until the
mixture thickens enough to coat the back of the spoon
Do not let the custard boil, or it will curdle. Serve hot.

bread & butter pudding

Serves **4**

Preparation time **15 minutes**, plus standing

Cooking time **30–40 minutes**

4 thin slices of **day-old white bread**

¼ cup **unsalted butter**, plus extra for greasing

⅓ cup **golden raisins**

2 tablespoons **candied peel** (optional)

grated **zest** of 1 **lemon**

1¼ cups **light cream** and 1¼ cups **milk** or 2½ cups **milk**

2 **eggs**, plus 2 **egg yolks**

2 tablespoons **granulated sugar**

½ teaspoon freshly grated **nutmeg**

1–2 tablespoons **jelly marmalade**, heated

Spread the bread slices with the butter and cut each into 4 triangles. Place a layer of bread in the base of a greased 4 cup pie dish. Sprinkle the golden raisins, candied peel, if using, and lemon zest over the top and cover with the remaining bread triangles.

Beat the cream, if using, with the milk, eggs, egg yolks, and sugar in a bowl. Pour the mixture over the bread. Cover and allow to stand for 30 minutes.

Sprinkle the nutmeg over the surface and bake in a preheated oven, 350°F, for 30–40 minutes.

Remove from the oven and brush the hot marmalade over the top. Serve hot, with cream or stewed fruit, if desired.

For stewed summer berries to serve with the pudding, put 3½ cups mixed summer berries, such as blackberries, black currants, and raspberries, ¼ cup superfine sugar, pared zest and juice of ½ lemon, and ¼ teaspoon ground allspice in a large saucepan. Heat gently until the sugar has dissolved, then simmer over a very low heat for 5–10 minutes until the fruits are softened and juicy.

tiramisu with white chocolate

Serves **4**

Preparation time **10 minutes,**
plus chilling

6 tablespoons freshly made
black coffee, cooled

3 tablespoons **Frangelico**

4 oz store-bought **sponge
cake**

1¾ cups **heavy cream**

2 tablespoons **confectioners'
sugar**

3 **egg whites**

½ cup grated **white
chocolate**

Combine the coffee and Frangelico. Cut the sponge
cake into cubes and divide half the cubes between
4 glasses. Add a tablespoon of the coffee mixture to
each glass.

Whip the cream with the sugar and half the remaining
coffee mixture in a bowl until soft peaks form.

Beat the egg whites in a separate bowl until stiff, then
carefully fold into the cream mixture.

Spoon half the cream mixture into the glasses and top
with the remaining sponge cubes, coffee mixture, and
cream mixture. Sprinkle with the chocolate. Chill in the
refrigerator for 1 hour.

For raspberry & dark chocolate tiramisu, combine
the coffee as above with 3 tablespoons kirsch. Divide
the sponge cake cubes between 4 glasses, then
add a tablespoon of the coffee mixture and a few
fresh raspberries to each. Make the cream mixture
and assemble the desserts as above. Add 3 more
raspberries to each, then sprinkle over ½ cup grated
bittersweet chocolate.

fruit salad with elderflower syrup

Serves **4**

Preparation time **5 minutes**, plus cooling & standing

Cooking time **5 minutes**

⅔ cup **orange juice**

3 tablespoons **elderflower syrup**

1 **vanilla bean**, split lengthwise

1¾ cups **fresh blueberries**

1⅓ cups **fresh strawberries**, hulled and halved

1⅔ cups **fresh raspberries**

1 cup **seedless grapes**

2 **oranges**, segmented

Combine the orange juice, elderflower syrup, and vanilla bean in a saucepan and heat gently until just boiling. Reduce the heat and simmer gently for 5 minutes. Remove the pan from the heat and allow to cool for 30 minutes.

Put all the fruits in a bowl and mix together gently. Add the syrup mixture and allow to stand for 15 minutes. Serve in bowls with shortbread cookies.

For rose water & honey fruit salad, place 3 tablespoons honey, ⅔ cup cold water, and 1–2 tablespoons rose water in a saucepan and heat gently until just boiling. Reduce the heat and simmer gently for 5 minutes. Remove the pan from the heat and allow to cool for 30 minutes. Pour over the combined fruits as above and serve decorated with rose petals.

bananas en papillote

Serves **4**

Preparation time
2–3 minutes

Cooking time **3–4 minutes**

butter, for greasing
4 small firm **bananas**
1 **cinnamon stick**, cut into
  quarters
4 **star anise**
1 **vanilla bean**, cut into
  quarters
2 tablespoons **grated carob**
5 tablespoons **pineapple
  juice**

Lightly grease 4 pieces of foil or waxed paper, each large enough to wrap a banana. Put a banana in the center and add a piece of cinnamon stick, 1 star anise, and a piece of vanilla bean.

Sprinkle each with a quarter of the carob and pineapple juice. Seal the edges of the foil or paper together to form parcels.

Transfer the parcels to a baking sheet and bake in a preheated oven, 450°F, for 3–4 minutes. Alternatively, cook on top of a preheated barbecue or by the side of a bonfire—in both cases, use double-thickness foil to prevent splits and spillages. Serve with crème fraîche or mascarpone cheese.

For bananas with toffee & pecan sauce, heat ⅓ cup unsalted butter, ⅓ cup maple syrup, and ⅓ cup heavy cream in a saucepan over a low heat until the butter has melted. Increase the heat and simmer briskly for 5 minutes until the sauce has thickened. Stir in ½ cup chopped toasted pecan nuts and simmer for 1 minute more. Set aside to cool for 15–20 minutes. Serve the sauce warm drizzled over 4 peeled and sliced ripe bananas, or over bananas cooked with the spices as above.

caramel ice cream cake

Serves **8–10**

Preparation time **10 minutes**, plus standing, chilling, & freezing

4 cups **good-quality vanilla ice cream**

3 cups crushed **graham crackers**

⅓ cup **butter**, melted

7 oz **soft butterscotch fudge**

2 tablespoons **light cream**

Remove the ice cream from the freezer and let stand at room temperature for 30–45 minutes until it is well softened.

Meanwhile, put the crushed crackers in a bowl, add the melted butter, and mix together until the crumbs are moistened. Press the crumb mixture into a 9 inch round springform pan, pressing it up the edge of the pan to give a 1 inch side. Chill in the refrigerator for 20 minutes.

Put the fudge and cream in a saucepan and heat gently, stirring, until the fudge has melted. Carefully spread two-thirds of the fudge mixture over the crumb shell. Spoon the ice cream over the top and level the surface.

Drizzle the remaining caramel over the ice cream with a spoon and freeze for 4 hours. Unmold the cake and serve in wedges.

For a chocolate & caramel cake, make the crumb shell as above, but use 3 cups crushed chocolate coated cookies or chocolate cookies. Melt the fudge with the cream as above, then stir in 1 cup toasted ground hazelnuts. Pour all the mixture into the crumb base, then top with the softened vanilla ice cream. Melt 2 oz semisweet chocolate in a heatproof bowl set over a saucepan of gently simmering water (don't let the bowl touch the water). Drizzle over the ice cream and freeze as above.

nectarine brûlée

Serves **6**
Preparation time **10 minutes**
Cooking time **10–15 minutes**

1 lb **nectarines**, pitted and
 sliced
4 tablespoons **orange
 liqueur**, plus extra to flavor
 the fruit
1½ cups **sour cream**
pinch of freshly grated
 nutmeg
1 teaspoon **vanilla extract**
½ cup **light brown sugar**

Put the nectarines in a saucepan and add enough water
to cover. Poach over a low heat for 5–10 minutes, or
until tender. Drain and divide between 6 individual
ramekins. Stir in a little orange liqueur.

Beat together the sour cream, nutmeg, vanilla extract,
and the 4 tablespoons orange liqueur in a bowl until well
combined. Spoon over the nectarine slices, then sprinkle
the sugar over the top in a thick layer.

Cook under a preheated high broiler until the sugar
caramelizes. Serve with brandy snaps, langues du chat,
or amaretti cookies.

For lemon cookies to serve with the brûlée, put
½ cup softened butter, ¼ cup superfine sugar, grated
zest of 1 lemon, and ½ tablespoon lemon juice in a
bowl. Using an electric hand-held mixer, beat together
until pale and light. Sift in 1¼ cups self-rising flour and
continue beating to form a stiff dough. Take walnut-size
pieces of the dough, roll into balls, and flatten into
2 inch discs. Place on a large baking sheet lined with
parchment paper and bake in a preheated oven, 350°F,
for 12–15 minutes until lightly golden. Allow to cool on
the baking sheet for 5 minutes, then transfer to a
cooling rack to cool completely.

easy chocolate fudge cake

Makes **12 portions**
Preparation time **10 minutes**
Cooking time **50–55 minutes**

8 oz **semisweet chocolate**,
 broken into pieces
1 cup **butter**, plus extra
 for greasing
4 **eggs**, beaten
½ cup **superfine sugar**
2 cups **self-rising flour**,
 sifted

Frosting
6 oz **semisweet chocolate**,
 broken into pieces
⅔ cup **light cream**

Grease an 8 x 12 inch baking pan and line the base with parchment paper. Put the chocolate and butter in a heatproof bowl set over a saucepan of gently simmering water (don't let the bowl touch the water) and stir over a low heat until melted. Allow to cool for 5 minutes.

Meanwhile, using an electric hand-held mixer, beat together the eggs and sugar in a bowl for 5 minutes until thick. Beat in the cooled chocolate mixture and fold in the flour.

Spoon the mixture into the prepared pan and bake in a preheated oven, 325°F, for 45–50 minutes until risen and firm to the touch. Allow to cool in the pan for 10 minutes, then turn out onto a cooling rack to cool completely, removing the paper from the base.

Meanwhile, make the frosting. Put the chocolate in a saucepan with the cream and heat gently, stirring, until the chocolate has melted. Allow to cool for 1 hour until thickened to a pouring consistency, then spread over the cake. Allow to set for 30 minutes before serving.

For chocolate butter frosting, instead of the cream frosting, beat together 1¾ cups softened butter, 1 cup confectioners' sugar, and ½ cup sifted cocoa powder in a bowl until evenly combined. Spread over the cake and serve topped with ½ cup grated semisweet chocolate curls.

chocolate refrigerator cake

Makes **30 fingers**
Preparation time **15 minutes**,
  plus chilling
Cooking time **5 minutes**

1 lb **semisweet chocolate**,
  broken into pieces
½ cup **unsalted butter**, plus
  extra for greasing
1 cup roughly crushed
  graham crackers
⅔ cup roughly chopped
  dried figs
½ cup **dried cranberries**
½ cup **hazelnuts**, toasted
⅓ cup **almonds**, toasted and
  roughly chopped
confectioners' sugar, for
  dusting (optional)

Grease a 7 x 9 inch rectangular cake pan and line
the base with parchment paper. Put the chocolate
and butter in a heatproof bowl set over a saucepan of
gently simmering water (don't let the bowl touch the
water) and stir over a low heat until melted. Stir in all
the remaining ingredients.

Spoon the mixture into the prepared pan. Press well
into the base and sides of the pan and smooth the
surface with a spatula.

Cover with foil and chill for 4 hours or overnight in the
refrigerator. Carefully work round the edges of the cake
with the spatula and unmold onto a board, removing the
paper from the base. Dust with confectioners' sugar, if
desired, and serve in thin fingers.

For a white chocolate rocky road cake, put 12 oz
white chocolate, broken into pieces, in a bowl set
over a saucepan of gently simmering water (don't let
the bowl touch the water) and leave until melted.
Meanwhile, spray a 2 lb loaf pan with spray olive oil
and line with parchment paper. Stir 7 oz roughly
chopped Turkish delight (any flavor of your choice),
¾ cup shelled pistachio nuts, and ⅓ cup shredded
coconut into the melted chocolate. Pour the mixture
into the prepared pan, smooth the surface, and
refrigerate for 4 hours. Turn out, removing the
paper, and cut into slices to serve.

index

acknowledgments

Executive Editor: Nicola Hill
Editor: Amy Corbett
Executive Art Editor: Sally Bond
Designer: one2six creative limited
Photographer: Ian Wallace
Food and props stylist: Louise Pickford
Production Controller: Carolin Stransky

Commissioned photography: © Octopus Publishing Group Limited/Ian Wallace apart from the following: © Octopus Publishing Group Limited/David Jordan 19, 156; /Gareth Sambidge 63, 77, 127, 129, 131, 133, 139, 143, 145, 147, 161, 201, 227; /Ian Wallace 23, 27; /Sean Myers 33, 67, 165; /Simon Smith 137, 169, 178, 183, 186, 211, 220, 231; /William Reavell 59, 119, 194, 214; /William Lingwood 65.